SQUADRONS!

No. 8

The Handley Page
Halifax Mk. I

Phil H. Listemann

ISBN: 978-2918590-47-7

Copyright

© 2015 Philedition - Phil Listemann
updated August 2018

Colour profiles: Bill Dady

All right reserved. No part of this book may be reproduced, stored in a retrieval system or transmitted in any form by any means, electronic, mechanical, photocopying, recording or otherwise, without prior permission of the author.

Glossary of Terms

Personel :
(AUS)/RAF: Australian serving in the RAF
(BEL)/RAF: Belgian serving in the RAF
(CAN)/RAF: Canadian serving in the RAF
(CZ)/RAF: Czechoslovak serving in the RAF
(NFL)/RAF: Newfoundlander serving in the RAF
(NL)/RAF: Dutch serving in the RAF
(NZ)/RAF: New Zealander serving in the RAF
(POL)/RAF: Pole serving in the RAF
(RHO)/RAF: Rhodesian serving in the RAF
(SA)/RAF: South African serving in the RAF
(US)/RAF - RCAF : American serving in the RAF or RCAF

Ranks
G/C : Group Captain
W/C : Wing Commander
S/L : Squadron Leader
F/L : Flight Lieutenant
F/O : Flying Officer
P/O : Pilot Officer
W/O : Warrant Officer
F/Sgt : Flight Sergeant
Sgt : Sergeant
Cpl : Corporal
LAC : Leading Aircraftman

Other
ATA: Air Transport Auxiliary
CO : Commander
DFC : Distinguished Flying Cross
DFM : Distinguished Flying Medal
DSO : Distinguished Service Order
Eva. : Evaded
ORB : Operational Record Book
OTU : Operational Training Unit
PoW : Prisoner of War
PAF: Polish Air Force
RAF : Royal Air Force
RAAF : Royal Australian Air Force
RCAF : Royal Canadian Air Force
RNZAF : Royal New Zealand Air Force
SAAF : South African Air Force
s/d: Shot down
Sqn : Squadron
† : Killed

THE HALIFAX I

From before the end of the Great War the United Kingdom had coveted long-range bombers that were able to bomb the continent. Bomber Command, formed in 1936, was a major and vital organisation within the RAF. While the twin-engine Vickers Wellington was about to be introduced, a new generation of four-engine bombers was already under development. The concept was not new but, in the middle of the 1930s, technological progress with engines and airframe materials gave the opportunity for many air forces to develop their long-range bombers. It was also a matter of prestige as the long-range bomber, also known as the 'strategic' bomber, was not accessible to all. In the middle of the '30s, the USA and Germany had various projects under way (Germany gave up later on) and even Italy joined in. When the war broke out, the UK had two projects of 'strategic' bombers on the table (as required by British policy at the time in case one project failed) - the Short Stirling and the Handley Page Halifax.

The Halifax was designed in response to Air Ministry Specification B.12/36, issued in May 1936, calling for an all-metal, four-engine, mid-wing monoplane. Handley Page submitted its design (H.P. 57) and the Air Ministry ordered two prototypes, L7244 and L7245, in April 1937. L7244 was intended to be a pure test airframe and L7245 would be fully equipped for complete service trials. While studies were underway, an order for 100 Halifax Mk Is was placed in January 1938 with the serials as follows: **L9495-L9534, L9560-L9584, L9600-L9624.**

The first prototype, L7244, was completed on 2 September (the day before the United Kingdom declared war). The first flight was delayed and the aircraft moved to another base because of concerns it might be damaged or destroyed by the enemy. Its maiden flight, from RAF Bicester, was on 25 October.

After one year of testing, the first production Halifax Mk I flew on 11 October 1940. The mark received constant improvement and, under the denomination of Halifax Mk I, 85 aircraft in three series were produced:

Series 1: 39 of these were produced and delivered as followed: October 1940 (1), November 1940 (2), December 1940 (2), January 1941 (2), February 1941 (7), March 1941 (7), April 1941 (10), May 1941 (8), June 1941 (8), July 1941 (1). The 31st machine (L9515) was held by the manufacturer and served as the test-bed for the Mk II and equipped with Merlin XX engines.

The prototype HP.57 (L7244) seen without armament a few weeks after completion (the turrets substituted by metal fairings). After being test flown for more than a year, L7244 was briefly used as a trainer with 35 Sqn between November 1940 and August 1941. L7244 became an instructional airframe as 3299M in August 1942.

Series 2: 25 of these were delivered (L9560-L9584), with a strengthened structure allowing a new maximum take-off weight of 60,000 lb instead of 55,000 lb. They were also equipped with Vickers K-guns mounted in pairs to fire on the beam through side hatches amidships, so as to cover blind spots hidden from the nose and tails turrets' field of fire by the wing and tail unit. They were delivered as follows: June 1941 (7), July 1941 (5), August 1941 (7), September 1941 (6).

Series 3: The last nine were L9600-L9608 as the last 16 of the initial order were eventually delivered as Halifax Mk IIs. These nine Mk Is had deeper oil coolers installed to provide for Merlin XXs instead of Merlin Xs, an increased fuel capacity. Except for the engineers, these last Mk Is were actually very similar to the next mark, the Mk II, which would become the first major Halifax version built. The last Mk.Is were delivered as follows: August 1941 (1), September 1941 (2), October 1941 (5). However, it seems that Merlin XXs were sometime installed after 1942 during a major inspection, and not only on Series 3 aircraft, as it is confirmed that L9577, which served up to March 1944, has been such re-engined and re-named Halifax Mk II.

The Mk.I suffered from various shortcomings. In terms of defensive armament, there was no dorsal turret and the midships guns were basically useless. At maximum weight, the aircraft's ceiling was inadequate. Otherwise, ignoring the service ceiling, the Halifax was very close in performance to the American B-17C/D (which was not, however, considered as being fully combat ready), and also close to the E model.

With such a small number produced, the Halifax Mk.I could not become the main equipment of a large number of units. In the end, only two squadrons were fully equipped - No. 35 Squadron followed by No. 76. The number of sorties, less than 500, can also be seen as marginal. When compared with what the Halifax did for Bomber Command, close to 83,000 sorties (including over 73,000 bomber sorties), the 500 sorties of the Mk I can even be considered as insignificant but its impact was elsewhere. Indeed, despite its shortcomings, the Halifax proved it could be a great asset as a bomber for the RAF. The start was slow and difficult and losses were high (as was the case for any RAF bomber type in 1941-1942). On 1 January, 1942, when the Halifax Mk I was about to be withdrawn from operations, only 36, of the 86 taken on charge by the RAF, were still in flying condition. The Halifax reached maturity much later on in 1943 with the Mk.III but by that time the Lancaster had appeared and effectively sealed the fate of the Halifax in the general 'popular' face of history. The Halifax would for ever be overshadowed by the Lancaster.

The second prototype was fully equipped with its turrets: Nose - Boulton Paul Type B with two guns with 1,000 rpg; Tail – Boulton Paul Type C with 1,700 rpg and 4,000 more in reserve. As was usual at the time, L7245 had its undersides painted yellow. The photo below shows that the Halifax was a shaped aircraft. L7245 was intensively tested at A&AEE from 11.09.40 to 05.11.41 when it returned to Handley Page for overhaul before being allocated to 28 CF one month later. It was struck off charge on 28.02.42 and later converted to an instructional airframe as 3474M.

Halifax prototype L7245 taken during one of its test flights.

November 1940 – February 1942

Number of sorties: ca. 290

First operational sortie: 10.03.41
Last operational sortie: 10.01.42

Number of claims: 9
Total aircraft written-off: 26
Aircraft lost on operations: 23
Aircraft lost in accidents: 3

Squadron code letters:
TL

Commanding Officers

W/C Raymond W.P. Collins	RAF No. 24083	RAF	05.11.40	03.07.41
W/C Basil V. Robinson	RAF No. 34089	RAF	03.07.41	26.01.42
W/C John N.H. Whitworth	RAF No. 26249	RAF	26.01.42	...

Squadron Usage

For its first four-engine bomber, the RAF decided to re-form a squadron that had been disbanded the previous April (1940). No. 35 Squadron was placed under the command of Wing Commander R.W.P. Collins. At the same time the first pilots were posted in - S/L P.A. Gilchrist, F/L T.P.A. Bradley and F/Os M.T.G. Henry and R.V. Warren. All had a lot of experience on Whitleys and all had the DFC ribbon on their chest (Gilchrist and Bradley for their actions with 51 Sqn and Henry and Warren with 10 Sqn).
On the 13th, F/O Henry ferried the first Halifax to the squadron (L9486). The squadron moved, one week later, from Boscombe Down, where it had been re-formed, to Leeming and then to Linton-on-Ouse on 5 December. This station would remain its base for the next two years or so. In the meantime, the prototype, L7244, was temporarily taken on charge for training after being ferried in by the CO himself on 23 November.
Remaining under 4 Group authority, more pilots were provided in December - one from 51 Sqn (F/L G.A Lane DFC), two from 77 Sqn (P/O G.A.L Elliott DFC and L.J. Macdonald) and one each from 78 and 58 Squadrons (F/O E.G. Franklin and P/O T.D.I Robinson respectively). Three Sergeant pilots were also added (A. Woolnough from 77 Sqn and L. Bovington from 51, S.D. Graeves from 78). A third Halifax was received on 4 January (L9487) and a fourth (L9489) one week later on the 12th but the first dramatic accident occurred the following day when, during a fuel consumption test, L9487 crashed killing all in board. The captain was F/O Michael Henry who had previously served with No. 10 Sqn where he had earned the DFC in July 1940. The crew was also composed of one New Zealander, Leslie McDonald with 28 operations to his credit, and one Irishman, William Jesse, who had recently been awarded the DFM for his service with 58 Sqn. The reason for the crash was never established but eyewitnesses reported seeing the bomber flying at 8,000 feet (the bomber had to measure the fuel consumption at 12,000) with its undercarriage down and trailing smoke and flames. During the month, training continued for half a dozen crews. One more pilot arrived on the 26th, F/O J.L. Cheshire DSO from 102 Sqn, and, two days later, it was the turn of P/O W.S. Hilary

J.B. 'Willy' Tait served with 35 Sqn as Flight CO and Squadron Leader. He's seen here as a Wing Commander while he was commanding 617 Sqn when the squadron attacked and sunk the Tirpitz in Norway in November 1944.

Flying Officer Leonard Cheshire (middle) posing with other members of 35 Sqn. He was posted in for his second tour of operations. He became one of the most outstanding Bomber Command pilots and ended the war with the Victoria Cross (unusually awarded not for a single act but for four years of valour), the DSO and two bars and the DFC.

from 10 Sqn (where he had been awarded the DFM). On 1 February, L9493 was taken on charge followed by L9496 on the 15th and L9488 and L9490 the following day. During the end of the month, the squadron received more aircraft (L9498 and L9502) and crews (three from 10, three from 51, two from 58, four from 77 and one each from 78 and 102). In the first week of March the squadron carried out 66 hours of flight and two more Mk Is were added to the inventory, L9492 and L9499, and, on the 10th, L9504. That day the RAF decided it was time to try the Halifax on operations. A small-scale raid over Le Havre (docks and shipping canal) alongside eight Blenheims was a good introduction. During the briefing, a message was received from the AOC, passing on his good wishes to the crews for the first Halifax operation, proving that the Halifax, as did all of the British 'heavies', represented the hope that the war could be won by air-power alone. The first Halifax (L9486/B) took off at 19.00 flown by W/C Collins and within 20 minutes all of the serviceable Halifaxes were airborne. One aircraft (P/O J.M. Murray and crew) was unable to proceed due to a hydraulic failure. The weather was excellent and most of the aircraft were able to drop their bombs over Le Havre despite clouds from 10,000/12,000 feet. Only one aircraft could not drop its bombs over Le Havre - L9496/N flown by F/L Bradley – and diverted to Dieppe where the bombs were dropped from 12,000 feet. Flak was encountered but no damage was caused although L9493/G, flown by F/O Warren, suffered from one engine over-heating. The raid was considered successful. Sadly, on the return journey, Halifax L9489/F, flown by S/L Gilchrist, the B Flight Commander, was shot down by mistake by an RAF fighter over Surrey and all of the crewmen, except two (including Gilchrist), perished. A replacement Halifax, L9500, arrived two days later. The same night, the Halifaxes were called upon to attack a more ambitious target, in Germany this time, when they were tasked to be part of an 88 aircraft raid on the Blohm & Voss works at Hamburg. The three Halifaxes took off between 21.15 and 21.25 but, owing to failure of both turrets, L9496/N, flown by F/L Bradley, had to return early. The two others continued and delivered their bombs from around 13,000 feet. Inaccurate flak was encountered but F/L Lane's L9488/M was attacked by a German night fighter 30 miles north of the island of Norderney. The German aircraft gave up after four unsuccessful attacks on the Halifax. The following night the squadron returned, with two aircraft including one flown by the CO, to the same target with 137 other Bomber Command aircraft. Both aircraft returned safely after more than 5.5 hours in the air. No more operations were organised until the end of the month but the squadron continued to receive more crews and Halifaxes and completed more than 200 hours of training flights. By the end of the month more than 30 crews had been posted in with A Flight under the command of S/L J.B. Tait (a former 51 Sqn pilot with the DFC) and B Flight with S/L Gilchrist as CO.

Despite the positive activities in March, April wasn't an active month. More aircraft arrived but with some pilots posted out, and No. 76 Squadron formed from a third flight, only one raid was carried out that month. During the night of 15-16 April, five Halifaxes took off for Kiel and delivered attacks at heights between 9,500 and 11,000 feet. The squadron was part of a 100 aircraft raid but bombing was inaccurate owing to haze over the target. Heavy flak was encountered and L9493, captained by Sgt Lashbrook, was damaged over the target but the pilot was able to return to base. However, while circling the aerodrome, both port engines failed in succession and a forced landing was made on the two surviving engines in a field near Tollerton. The aircraft crashed into a tree and the crewmembers were slightly injured in the process. All of the remaining squadron aircraft returned safely to base.

In May, no raids were carried out as the squadron was involved in more training and demonstrations to show the new bomber to various authorities. The squadron, however, was lucky when, during the early hours of the 12th the station was attacked by German bombers. Many bombs hit the squadron facilities, one squadron ground crew (Cpl K.H Martloth) was killed and two others died from their wounds later on (AC2s H.H. Meeson and A. Dale). The Station Commander, G/C Frederick F. Garraway, was killed while conducting the fire fighting operations. On the positive side, none of the Halifaxes was destroyed or damaged. On 20 May, S/L Gilchrist was posted out to take command of the Canadian No. 405 Squadron and was replaced as B Flight CO by T. Bradley. Serious business restarted in June with no less than eight raids, representing 55 sorties, but operations didn't start until the night of 11/12th. Before that, routine duties were carried out. A demonstration for the Prime Minister on the 6th, however, was not routine. This took place at West Raynham with L9506 captained by the CO and his crew. The first operation of the month saw six Halifaxes, led by S/L Tait DSO, as part of an 80 bomber raid on Duisburg. They took off half an hour before midnight but the results of the raid were not observed because of haze and cloud obscuring the target. The Halifaxes dropped their bombs from heights between 7,000 and 15,500 feet. The next day, in company with seven Stirlings, eight Halifaxes were detailed to attack chemical works at Hulls. For this raid the new Station Commander, G/C Graham was on board S/L Bradley's Halifax (L9496/N). Owing to adverse weather, the target was only located and attacked by three Halifaxes which delivered their loads between 11,000 and 15,000 feet. One direct hit was observed. The remaining aircraft bombed secondary targets. On return, one engine of L9498 failed and the captain, Sgt L.W. Bovington, overshot on landing but no serious injuries were reported by the crew. All of the other aircraft returned safely to base even though two were attacked by German fighters during the journey home. L9500/Z (F/O James) was attacked from the rear. The rear gunner fired at the enemy fighter three times without result. The other fighter attack ended decisively with the rear gunner of L9492/X (Pilot - Sgt Clarence Godwin), Sgt Conrad Newstead, firing a 10-second burst and shooting the German aircraft down in flames south of the Zuider Zee. On the night of the 15/16th, 10 aircraft were despatched to Hanover. Owing to cloud, the target was not completely identified and the Halifaxes were obliged to descend, to between 8,000 and 14,000 feet, to deliver their bombs. F/O Franklin, flying L9508/F, bombed from 2,000 feet! One aircraft diverted to Osnabruck and another returned with its bombs. The aircraft flown by F/O Murray was attacked by a single-engine He113. One engine was hit, and had to be shut down, and the rear gunner was injured. However a burst from his guns forced the German to dive away. The aircraft was able to return to base where it crashed without causing any further injuries to the crew. It is worth noting that the second pilot, P/O David S.S. Wilkerson, would be posted to 58 Sqn the following month and became a Wing Commander with a DSO and DFC before he was killed in a flying accident on 16 September 1944 at the age of 27. The following night, 16/17 June, the squadron, led by the CO, detailed three Halifaxes to hit the same target. All returned safely to base and all of the bombs were seen to have hit the target area. The next raid – six aircraft to Kiel – was flown four nights later and was uneventful. The two following raids, again with six aircraft to Kiel on the night of 23/24 June and 26/27 June, were also relatively routine. However, during the latter, Sgt Godwin in L9495/B was intercepted by German fighters off Sylt but escaped by diving to low level while the gunners forced the Bf109s to stay a good distance away. The last raid of the month was carried out on the 30th and was the first daylight raid for the squadron as it joined 28 Blenheims of No. 2 Group. Kiel was the target again. The six Halifaxes, led by S/L Tait, took off at 10.00. Over the target the weather was perfect and they encountered heavy flak but that did not prevent the Halifaxes from dropping their bombs from 17-18,000 feet. However, enemy fighters soon showed up and attacked the Halifax flown by F/L Robinson (L9499/Q) on the return journey. The aircraft was last seen on fire but still resisting strongly and it is believed that the gunners shot down at least one of the attackers. Of the seven crewmen, all but one were killed. The surviving man became a PoW. L9499 was shot down by *Oblt* Walter Fenske of 3./NJG 1 for his 12th victory. Robinson's Halifax was not the only one to be attacked by German fighters. L9501/Y (F/O Owen) was also attacked by three Bf110s that made five single attacks on the Halifax causing serious damage and severely wounding the beam gunner, Sgt Alexander U. Simpson. Sadly, Simpson died during the flight home as the Halifax limped back on three engines. Two other crewmembers were also slightly wounded and one Bf110 was claimed as destroyed. L9501 landed at base at 16.00 without any further trouble.

Because of the generally good weather that summer, Bomber Command increased the number of raids in July and the squadron and its Halifaxes participated in nine of them. The first day of July began with good news for the personnel as they proudly celebrated the award of an immediate bar to the DSO of A Flight CO S/L Tait and the DFC to P/O Owen for their gallantry in the pre-

Halifax L9503 was a Mk I of the first series. Allocated to the Squadron on 23.02.41, it was sent on operations for the first time on the night 11/12 June 1941. This Halifax failed to return from Hamburg seven months later when on its 20th mission.

A crew boarding their Halifax Mk I, L9600/TL-U. From the last batch, L9600 was issued to the squadron on 15.10.41 and carried out its first mission on 7/8 November. It failed to return from a raid to Köln on 11/12 December. It was only its third operation.

vious day's daylight raid over Kiel. A second daytime raid was scheduled for 3 July but was soon cancelled due to bad weather. The next planned raid, by night, was not cancelled. Various targets were chosen that night by Bomber Command and involved more than 200 aircraft with the squadron providing nine aircraft, led by S/L Bradley, for a raid on Magdeburg. All nine attacked the target successfully and all returned to base safely. Two nights later, 10 Halifaxes were detailed to attack Frankfurt alongside three Stirlings but L9502/R failed to return from the raid. All of the crew survived to become PoWs. Despite this loss, the squadron despatched seven aircraft to attack the oil refineries of Leuna but the result was the same with another Halifax, L9521/Z, lost when it was shot down by a night fighter (*Ltn* August Geiger of III./NG 1) and crashed in the Netherlands killing four Dutch civilians. Of the crew, three were killed and four were made prisoners. L9500/H, flown by Sgt James, was hit by flak but returned. Otherwise the raid was rather uneventful for the remaining five Halifaxes. To compensate somewhat for these recent losses, an immediate DFM was awarded on the 9th, again for actions during the Kiel raid, to Sgt D.P. Hogg. The squadron returned to operations on the night of 13/14 July when seven aircraft were despatched to Hanover. If we except the unsuccessful head-on attack, near the target, by a German single-engine fighter on Halifax L9512/U flown by Sgt Greaves, the raid was carried out with success with no major damage to aircraft or crews. On the night of 19/20 July, the squadron detailed eight aircraft to Hanover. All returned safely but one, F/O Owen's L9501/V, was obliged to land at the satellite aerodrome of Bircham Newton after flying home from the target on three engines, while L9500/H, flown by F/O James, returned to base with small flak holes. The following raid to Mannheim on 21/22 July was uneventful. On the 24th the squadron was called upon to provide aircraft for a daylight raid on La Rochelle's La Pallice port. The target was the German battleship 'Scharnhorst'. It was a major raid with 150 bombers, including some from 2 Group, and a strong escort. The raid proved to be deadly for the squadron which lost one aircraft each to flak and fighters - L9527/M (F/Sgt Godwin, five killed, two PoWs) and L9512/U (F/Sgt S.D. Greaves, all PoWs). Seven of the eight surviving aircraft were also attacked by fighters with many receiving damage. Unfortunately, Sgt P. Bolton, the wireless operator for S/L Bradley's crew, died instantly after he was hit in the chest and the rear gunner of L9511/D (captained by W/O Holden), P/O H. Stone, a DFM recipient during his time with 58 Sqn was also killed. Other crewmen from two different aircraft also received light injuries. This combat was not one-sided however, as the tail gunner of F/O James' L9500/H, Sgt M.A Sachs, claimed the destruction of one fighter and two more probables. The gunners had to face no less than 20 German fighters during the raid. L9501/Y, flown by F/O Owen, was 'luckier' as it was only attacked 10 times and the rear gunner, Sgt H.R. Higgins, claimed one Bf109 destroyed as did Sgt F.W Hill, the rear gunner of F/L G. Elliott's L9508/X. The rear gunner of L9507/W (P/O P. Johnston), Sgt T.N. Sankey, did well too as he claimed one confirmed and one probable. All of the remaining Halifaxes returned to base with various degrees of damage and some on three engines. For this action, Bradley was awarded an immediate DSO, Owen an immediate DFC and Sachs and Higgins received an immediate DFM. No. 76 Squadron, the other Halifax Mk I unit at the time, also participated in the raid and lost two aircraft as well. The next day S/L Tait was replaced by S/L James H. Marks (formerly of 77 and 58 Sqns) and that night the squadron sent two Halifaxes (L9503/P, F/O Cheshire and L9507/W, P/O Cooper) to Berlin. The latter failed to return and all of the crew, including F/Sgt A.J. Heller (awarded the DFM in May 1940), were lost. A final raid for July was carried out (three aircraft to Cologne, 30/31 July) with nothing of worth to report. July had proven to be a bloody month for the squadron with the loss of five Halifaxes in 285 operational hours. Training had consumed another 179 hours and one Halifax on the 17th when its undercarriage jammed and it belly-landed at Linton-on-Ouse with no injury to the crew.

August began with four aircraft attacking Berlin. F/L Cheshire took off first at 22.00 in L9503/P. Despite intense and accurate flak, the bombs were delivered between 12,000 and 15,000 feet and the four aircraft returned safely to base after an average of seven hours in the air. The next raid (5/6 August – Karlsruhe) was uneventful as was the one on Essen (7/8 August) even though L9508/X (P/O Williams) was attacked and engaged by an enemy fighter that disappeared into cloud after its single attack. Both the aircraft and the crew were unharmed. On 11 August, the squadron stopped training its own crews because of the formation of a Halifax Conversion Flight. Some crewmen had to be posted to this new unit, however. On the night of 12/13 August, a raid of 70 aircraft was organised to bomb Berlin. The squadron provided five Halifaxes and another two for a separate raid on Essen. Over the target, L9497/K was hit by flak that damaged one of its engines. At the same time, the pilot, P/O McGregor-Cheers had to take violent evasive action to avoid searchlights. He was successful but not without higher fuel consumption. The trouble were not over for the crew, however, as it was soon attacked by two night fighters. The German aircraft did not press home their attacks and the Halifax was able to escape without further damage. Soon afterwards, the damaged engine died and the Halifax reached the English coast, with the fuel gauges close to zero, and had to make a forced landing. All but one of the crew escaped major injuries but the aircraft was only good for spare parts. If L9497 was lucky enough to return, L9500/H, flown by P/O Lisle, and crew, was posted missing during a raid on Magdeburg (14/15 August). There were no survivors. During this raid, P/O Johnston's L9526/O was attacked by a Bf110 but was not damaged. The next two raids, Cologne (16/17 August) and Kiel (19/20th), were uneventful, but, on the Dusseldorf raid of the 24/25th, the squadron lost another Halifax. L9572/G and the crew of P/O McGregor-Cheers, who had survived flak, searchlights, night fighters and a forced landing due to low fuel less than a fortnight before, were all lost. Four nights later (28/29th), on a raid to Duisburg, the same fate befell P/O Adkins and his crew. Nine more sorties were carried out before the end of the month but, fortunately, no casualties were reported. In all, for August, more than 300 operational hours were flown.

September was a bloody month for the squadron despite less operational flying and hours completed (28 and 175 respectively). The month began on the night of the 2/3rd with a disastrous raid on Berlin by five aircraft but with only one succeeding in attacking the target (L9566/R - F/O Williams). Of the remainder, one was forced to return early due to engine trouble (L9504/H - Sgt Norman), another bombed Lubeck as it was unable to reach Berlin due to excessive fuel consumption (L9569/X – Sgt Hamilton) and two were posted missing (L9508/X – F/O R. James, two killed and five PoWs, and L9560/F – P/O D.S. Fraser, five killed and two PoWs). Among the crewmembers lost was P/O John Cushion. He was the son of AVM Cushion (AOC No. 40 Group). The squadron returned to Berlin five nights later as part of a major raid of close to 200 bombers. Three bombers were able to deliver their bombs to the target and all five 35 Sqn Halifaxes returned to base safely less the tail gunner, Sgt Jackson, of L9504/H (Sgt Norman). The captain had decided to divert to Kiel, being behind schedule, but, for unknown reasons, the Halifax went into a spin. Thinking that he would be unable to regain control, Norman gave the order to 'stand by to bale out' and jettisoned the bombs before he managed to right the aircraft. However, soon afterwards, it was discovered that Jackson had baled out, presumably having only heard the words "bale out". Three nights later (11/12th), the target chosen for the squadron was the city of Turin in Italy. Three aircraft were detailed and, unfortunately, another loss occurred when L9566/R was posted missing on its return journey after being last plotted north of Le Havre at 06.15. All of F/O G.S. Williams' crew became prisoners. L9526/O, flown by P/O Creswell, was luckier as it was obliged to make a forced-landing in England due to a shortage of fuel. The aircraft was declared damaged beyond repair. Two Halifaxes participated in a raid to Brest without loss (13/14 September) but on the next raid, to Hamburg (15/16 September), one more aircraft, L3503/P, was lost. One member of F/O H.J. Brown's crew was killed and the survivors became PoWs. The rest of the month was uneventful even though the squadron took part in two more raids (19/20th and 29/30th).

Brest in France, Essen, Nuremberg (twice), Wilhelmshaven, Bremen, Mannheim and Hamburg were the targets the squadron attacked during October. The month saw more sorties (34) and more operational and training hours (187 and 118 respectively) than all those before it. Losses were, happily, limited to just one aircraft lost, L9579/F (Sgt Williams), which was abandoned after running low on fuel returning from Nuremberg. In the middle of the month, S/L S.A. Middleton arrived from 58 Sqn to act as A Flight Commander. His arrival was most welcome as many experienced officers had been posted since August. The other major event in October was the arrival of the first two Halifax Mk IIs, R9364 and V9979, on the 24th but the Mk I continued to be supplied to the squadron at the same time. The end of the operational usage of the Mk I, however, was close...

Despite widespread bad weather in northern Europe in November, operations were maintained, but, of course, bombing accuracy suffered. Losses continued. L9603/P – P/O G. Whitaker – was shot down by *Oblt* Herbert Lütje of NJG 1 right after having attacked the target (Essen). Three of the crew were killed and four made prisoners. It was a major effort for Bomber Command, with the main target being the German capital, which sent close to 400 bombers that night (including seven from 35 Sqn) but was also costly as 37 bombers failed to return (close to a 10 per cent loss). The next two raids (Hamburg and Brest) were completed with one more loss for the squadron (L9582/T – F/Sgt J.C. Hamilton) during the raid on the former. That month the squadron used the Mk II for the first time, on 25 November, when one of the new Halifaxes accompanied six Mk Is that night. In December there was little activity with the squadron providing two aircraft for a raid on Aachen, on the night of 7/8th, and five more to Cologne four nights later. Sgt Grigg and crew were posted missing in L9600 on this raid and would be the last operational Mk I loss for the squadron. It was actually the last raid the squadron's Mk Is flew in numbers as the last two raids of the year, daylight raids to Brest, were carried out by Mk IIs which were now fully operational. The Mk Is' war was not over, however, as they flew three more raids in January alongside the squadron's Mk IIs. The last raid was carried out on the night of the 10/11th to Wilhelmshaven. Since March 1941, the squadron had carried out 289 sorties on the Halifax Mk I and had lost 23 aircraft on operations - a high rate of 12.5 per cent.

Summary of the aircraft lost on Operations - 35 Squadron

T/O Date	Pilot	S/N	Origin	Serial	Code	Fate
10.03.41	S/L Peter A. **Gilchrist**	RAF No. 37348	RAF	**L9487**	TL-F	-
	Sgt Reginald **Lucas**	RAF No. 741992	RAF			†
	Sgt Ronald G. **Aedy**	RAF No. 568825	RAF			inj.
	P/O Edward R. **Arnold**	RAF No. 77908	RAF			†
	Sgt Stanley **Broadhurst**	RAF No. 550817	RAF			†
	F/O Albert E. **Cooper**	RAF No. 77963	RAF			†
16.04.41	Sgt Wallace I. **Lashbrook**	RAF No. 563198	RAF	**L9493**	TL-G	-
	Sgt Alfred R. **Robbins**	RAF No. 754051	RAF			-
	Sgt Cyril A. **Hewlett**	RAF No. 1267271	RAF			-
	Sgt **Somerville**	?	?			-
	Sgt Charles M. **Muir**	RAF No. 1005864	RAF			-
	Sgt **Broadbent**	?	?			-
13.06.41	Sgt Lionel W. **Bovington**	RAF No. 566881	RAF	**L9498**	TL-T	-
	Sgt Ronald **Mederith**	RAF No. 937585	RAF			-
	P/O Arthur G. **Eperon**	RAF No. 84713	RAF			-
	Sgt Albert E. **Hammond**	RAF No. 535641	RAF			-
	Sgt Reginald T. **Rudlin**	RAF No. 912084	RAF			-
	Sgt Noel E. H. **Coleman**	RAF No. 1107286	RAF			-
	Sgt Norman **Willingham**	RAF No. 922470	RAF			-
16.06.41	F/O James W. **Murray**	RAF No. 740164	RAF	**L9506**	TL-X	-
	P/O David S.S. **Wilkerson**	RAF No. 62281	RAF			-
	Sgt Robert W. **Nixon**	RAF No. 534331	RAF			-
	Sgt Ernest W. **Constable**	RAF No. 654498	RAF			-
	Sgt Douglas J. **Mennie**	RAF No. 940550	RAF			-
	Sgt Richard **Martin**	RAF No. 1076885	RAF			-
	Sgt John **Colgan**	RAF No. 532713	RAF			-
30.06.41	F/L Thomas D.I. **Robison**	RAF No. 42768	(NZ)/RAF	**L9499**	TL-Q	†
	Sgt Laurence **Hancock**	RAF No. 977649	RAF			†
	Sgt Percy **Ingham**	RAF No. 526092	RAF			†
	Sgt Ernest J. **Harding**	RAF No. 747842	RAF			PoW
	F/Sgt Alexander J. **Davie**	RAF No. 620056	RAF			†
	Sgt Richard N. **Hares**	RAF No. 1113461	RAF			†
	Sgt Robert **Dunn**	RAF No. 1109715	RAF			†
07.07.41	F/O Peter **Langmead**	RAF No. 86629	RAF	**L9502**	TL-R	PoW
	Sgt William T. **Hogan**	RAF No. 1051895	RAF			PoW
	Sgt Frederick H. **Brown**	RAF No. 1160266	RAF			PoW
	Sgt George **Roberts**	RAF No. 581189	RAF			PoW
	Sgt Ronald F. **Jackson**	RAF No. 550310	RAF			PoW
	Sgt Kenneth **Cattran**	RAF No. 922326	RAF			PoW
	Sgt Kenneth **Hartland**	RAF No. 1020825	RAF			PoW
08.07.41	Sgt Lionel W. **Bovington**	RAF No. 566881	RAF	**L9521**	TL-Z	PoW
	Sgt Thomas A. **Parkes**	RAF No. 526677	RAF			†
	Sgt Archie R. **Kiddey**	RAF No. 1151315	RAF			PoW
	F/Sgt George D. **Barry**	RAF No. 580820	RAF			PoW
	F/Sgt Albert E. **Hammond**	RAF No. 535641	RAF			†
	Sgt Henry S. **Bradbeer**	RAF No. 805520	RAF			PoW
	Sgt Noel E. H. **Coleman**	RAF No. 1107286	RAF			†
24.07.41	F/Sgt Stanley D. **Greaves**	RAF No. 754271	RAF	**L9512**	TL-U	PoW
	Sgt John N. **Gibson**	RAF No. 914683	RAF			PoW

	Sgt Gordon H.F. Ogden	RAF No. 569526	RAF			**PoW**
	Sgt Wilfrid C. Walters	RAF No. 581003	RAF			**PoW**
	Sgt Albert Henery	RAF No. 936275	RAF			**PoW**
	Sgt Ernest W. Constable	RAF No. 654498	RAF			**PoW**
	Sgt Allan Gillbanks	RAF No. 1115193	RAF			**PoW**
	F/Sgt Clarence A. Godwin	RAF No. 745859	RAF	L9527	TL-M	†
	Sgt Greville G. Esnouf	RAF No. 929408	RAF			†
	Sgt Conrad H. Newstead	RAF No. 567204	RAF			†
	P/O Arthur G. Eperon	RAF No. 84713	RAF			**PoW**
	Sgt Eric O.T. Balcomb	RAF No. 968379	RAF			**PoW**
	Sgt Reginald T. Rudlin	RAF No. 912084	RAF			†
	F/Sgt Sidney H.J. Shirley	RAF No. 804422	RAF			†
26.07.41	P/O Ernest R.P.S. Cooper	RAF No. 87050	RAF	L9507	TL-W	†
	Sgt John M.R. Cruickshank	RAF No. 1051632	RAF			†
	Sgt Ernest Short	RAF No. 567019	RAF			†
	F/Sgt Robert V. Collinge	RAF No. 581204	RAF			†
	F/Sgt Albert J. Heller	RAF No. 552112	RAF			†
	Sgt Douglas J. Mennie	RAF No. 940550	RAF			†
	F/Sgt Reginald A. Bates	RAF No. 751214	RAF			†
13.08.41	P/O Jack McGregor-Cheers	RAF No. 64889	RAF	L9497	TL-K	-
	Sgt Thomas A. Burne	Can./ R.74116	RCAF			inj.
	Sgt Walter N. Collins	RAF No. 617140	RAF			-
	Sgt Alistair A.S. Heggie	RAF No. 967663	RAF			-
	Sgt Jack Fuller	RAF No. 987503	RAF			-
	Sgt James B. Anderson	Can./R.54021	RCAF			-
	P/O Vivian M. Markham	RAF No. 100032	RAF			-
14.08.41	P/O Ronald Lisle	RAF No. 100618	RAF	L9500	TL-H	†
	Sgt Michael G. Garner	RAF No. 1168520	RAF			†
	Sgt Howard T. McQuigg	RAF No. 575079	RAF			†
	Sgt Kenneth R. Sewell	RAF No. 751350	RAF			†
	F/Sgt John J. Rogers	RAF No. 966861	RAF			†
	F/Sgt John A.A. Cox	RAF No. 648868	RAF			†
	Sgt Wallace L. Berry	Can./ R.59127	RCAF			†
25.08.41	P/O Jack McGregor-Cheers	RAF No. 64889	RAF	L9572	TL-G	†
	Sgt Thomas P. McHale	RAF No. 936804	RAF			†
	Sgt Walter N. Collins	RAF No. 617140	RAF			†
	Sgt Alistair A.S. Heggie	RAF No. 967663	RAF			†
	Sgt Jack Fuller	RAF No. 987503	RAF			†
	Sgt James B. Anderson	Can./ R.54021	RCAF			†
	P/O Vivian M. Markham	RAF No. 100032	RAF			†
28.08.41	P/O Arthur E.C. Adkins	RAF No. 101039	RAF	L9501	TL-Y	†
	P/O Charles J. Pearson	RAF No. 64268	RAF			†
	Sgt Frederick W. Hill	RAF No. 902598	RAF			†
	Sgt Harold Brelsford	RAF No. 1162052	RAF			†
	Sgt Alfred J. Manning	RAF No. 961238	RAF			†
	Sgt Herbert Thompson	RAF No. 1052413	RAF			†
	Sgt Alfred W. Rose	RAF No. 746835	RAF			†
02.09.41	F/O Ross James	RAF No. 42062	RAF	L9508	TL-X	†
	Sgt Stewart R. Arthur	RAF No. 1256692	RAF			**PoW**
	Sgt Albert R.P. Mills	RAF No. 702480	RAF			**PoW**
	Sgt Harold S. Oldman	RAF No. 755756	RAF			**PoW**
	Sgt John K. Young	RAF No. 947403	RAF			†
	Sgt Rodney G. Mullally	RAF No. 975341	RAF			**PoW**
	Sgt Thomas F. Allanson	RAF No. 1019019	RAF			**PoW**
	P/O Douglas S. Fraser	RAF No. 88869	RAF	L9560	TL-F	†
	Sgt Robin L.B. Beare	RAF No. 1375044	RAF			**PoW**
	Sgt Norman Willingham	RAF No. 922470	RAF			†
	P/O John P.B. Cushion	RAF No. 88456	RAF			†

Date	Name	Service No.	Force	Aircraft	Code	Fate
	Sgt Denis **Slater**	RAF No. 755528	RAF			†
	Sgt Arthur H. **Stroud**	RAF No. 909968	RAF			†
	Sgt Edward **Wilkinson**	RAF No. 1018131	RAF			PoW
11.09.41	P/O Edmund K. **Creswell**	RAF No. 107461	RAF	L9526	TL-O	-
	Sgt Douglas **Rowley-Blake**	RAF No. 1052303	RAF			-
	Sgt C.F. **Stewart**	?	?			-
	P/O Alfred **Abels**	RAF No. 65517	RAF			-
	Sgt Walter M.G. **Wing**	RAF No. 944314	RAF			-
	Sgt **Turner**	?	?			-
	Sgt **Lowe**	?	?			-
	F/O Gerald S. **Williams**	RAF No. 43051	RAF	L9566	TL-R	PoW
	Sgt Alexander **Osborne**	RAF No. 1265234	RAF			PoW
	Sgt John E. **Murrell**	RAF No. 801497	RAF			PoW
	P/O James O. **Hedley**	RAF No. 70295	RAF			PoW
	Sgt Charles F.S. **Ryder**	RAF No. 947433	RAF			PoW
	Sgt Ernest H. **Jackson**	RAF No. 1305759	RAF			PoW
	Sgt Alexander **Urquhart**	RAF No. 1118546	RAF			PoW
15.09.41	P/O Harold S. **Brown**	RAF No. 108027	RAF	L9503	TL-P	†
	S/L John H. **Barrett**	RAF No. 36091	RAF			PoW
	Sgt James W. **Hays**	RAF No. 568588	RAF			PoW
	F/Sgt John A. **Arnsby**	Can./ R.63675	RCAF			PoW
	Sgt Henry E. **Greene**	RAF No. 937497	RAF			PoW
	Sgt Ronald C. **Shaw**	RAF No. 951896	RAF			PoW
	Sgt Sydney T. **Fisher**	Can./ R.58473	RCAF			PoW
13.10.41	Sgt Harry A. **Williams**	RAF No. 937280	RAF	L9579	TL-P	-
	Sgt **Stocker**	?	?			-
	P/O L.M. **Mason**	?	?			-
	Sgt **Sykes**	?	?			-
	Sgt **Thorpe**	?	?			-
	Sgt Frank W. **Crocker**	RAF No.911566	RAF			-
	Sgt **Pennell**	?	?			-
07.11.41	P/O Gordon **Whitaker**	RAF No. 45055	RAF	L9603	TL-P	†
	Sgt Richard R. **Drummond**	RAF No. 925696	RAF			PoW
	Sgt Eric R. **Thomas**	RAF No. 618140	RAF			†
	Sgt Arthur R. **Kilminster**	RAF No. 962982	RAF			PoW
	Sgt Robert F. **Thompson**	RAF No. 974372	RAF			†
	F/Sgt Charles R. **Witcher**	Can./ R.59027	RCAF			PoW
	F/O Maurice O. **Stephens**	NZ403779	RNZAF			PoW
30.11.41	F/Sgt John C. **Hamilton**	RAF No. 969499	RAF	L9582	TL-T	PoW
	P/O Clifford G. **Lythgoe**	RAF No. 104493	RAF			PoW
	Sgt Walter R. **Stapleford**	RAF No. 569963	RAF			PoW
	Sgt Jeffrey A. **Longford**	RAF No. 956444	RAF			PoW
	Sgt Albert E. **Connor**	RAF No. 970956	RAF			PoW
	Sgt James P. **Henderson**	RAF No. 974000	RAF			PoW
	F/Sgt John **Collins**	RAF No. 905359	RAF			†
11.12.41	P/O Hubert D. **Buckley**	RAF No. 104512	RAF	L9600	TL-U	†
	Sgt Gerald L. **Grigg**	RAF No. 1165305	RAF			†
	Sgt Robert W.G. **Kent**	RAF No. 559083	RAF			†
	F/Sgt Ian R. **Bell**	RAF No. 581312	RAF			†
	Sgt Frank W. **Crocker**	RAF No. 911566	RAF			†
	Sgt Maurice V. **Wakeling**	RAF No. 1152209	RAF			†
	Sgt Laurence W. **Ketteringham**	RAF No. 1153499	RAF			†

Total: 23

Summary of the aircraft lost by accident - 35 Squadron

T/O Date	Pilot (and crew when available)	S/N	Origin	Serial	Code	Fate
13.01.41	F/O Michael T.G. **Henry**	RAF No. 39876	RAF	L9487		†
	P/O Leslie J. **McDonald**	RAF No. 79513	(NZ)/RAF			†
	Sgt John N. **Hall**	RAF No. 743002	RAF			†
	Sgt Anthony C.H.R. **Russell**	RAF No. 904441	RAF			†
	Sgt William C.B. **Jesse**	RAF No. 633777	(IRE)/RAF			†
	Sgt Francis L. **Plowman**	RAF No. 567918	RAF			†
17.07.41	*No details available*			L9490		-
	S/L James B. **Tait**	RAF No. 33291	RAF	L9495		-

Total: 3

Halifax beam gunners in position, introduced with Series 2. They wear an electrically heated flying suit. The leads, plugged into the aircraft's electrical system, can be seen running over the shoulder of the first gunner. Drums of ammunition are stacked in trays by each gunner. The overhead tracks carry ammunition to the rear turret.

Claims - 35 Squadron (Confirmed and Probable)

Date	Capt of the crew	SN	Origin	Type	Serial	Code	Nb	Cat.
13.06.41	Sgt Clarence A. **Godwin**	RAF No. 745859	RAF	Bf110	L9492	TL-X	1.0	C
27.06.41	P/O Robert F. **Owen**	RAF No. 88466	RAF	Bf110	L9501	TL-Y	1.0	C
24.07.41	F/O Peter S. **James**	RAF No. 83276	RAF	Bf109	L9500	TL-H	1.0	C
				Bf109			2.0	P
	F/O Robert F. **Owen**	RAF No. 88466	RAF	Bf109	L9501	TL-Y	1.0	C
	F/L George A.L. **Elliott**	RAF No. 43830	RAF	Bf109	L9508	TL-X	1.0	C
	P/O Peter **Johnston**	RAF No. 68139	RAF	Bf109	L9507	TL-W	1.0	C
				Bf109			1.0	P

Total: 9.0

May 1941 — February 1942

Number of sorties: ca. 150

First operational sortie: 14.07.41
Last operational sortie: 07.01.42

Number of claims: 2
Total aircraft written-off: 17
Aircraft lost on operations: 13
Aircraft lost in accidents: 4

Squadron code letters:
MP

Commanding Officers				
W/C Geoffrey T. Jarman	RAF No. 29211	RAF	28.05.41	01.09.41
W/C John J.A. Sutton	RAF No. 32114	RAF	01.09.41	15.12.41
W/C David O. Young	RAF No. 70764	RAF	15.12.41	...

Squadron Usage

After having served as an OTU in No. 6 Group between September 1939 and April 1940, and eventually being absorbed into No. 16 OTU, No. 76 Squadron was reformed at Linton-on-Ouse on 1 May 1941 and became the second Halifax bomber squadron. No. 35 Sqn had been informed two weeks previously to prepare its C Flight to become the A Flight of the future 76 Sqn. However, the working up was slow and by the end of the month only three crews had arrived - one from 35 Sqn (P/O W.S. Hillary) and two from 78 Sqn, a Whitley unit (P/O A.E. Lewin and P/O T.C. Richards). The CO, W/C G.T. Jarman, previously with No. 77 Squadron, arrived at the squadron to take command on the 28th. The first of the Halifaxes arrived on 3 May (L9516), followed by L9518 on the 5th, L9519 on the 8th, L9510, L9517 and L9523 on 12 May and L9514 on the 25th. Work-up continued until 4 June and the squadron moved to Middleton St. George to start operations against Germany. Only one flight was operational at the time and the squadron would only become fully operational by mid-June. The Halifax continued to be introduced progressively into the squadron with L9528, L9529 and L9530 arriving on 6 June, L9531 the next day, L9488 on 10 June, L9532 on the 12th, L9533 on the 14th, L9534 on the 15th, L9492 and L9496 on the 19th and L9494 the following day. Despite being half operational, the squadron had its baptism of fire when it participated in a raid on the night of 12/13 June. Three aircraft were sent to Essen and Hulls but the outcome was poor. F/L Hillary (L9516) and P/O Lewin (L9514) were both forced to return owing to engine trouble. Only P/O Richards was able to reach the target, Essen, but was unable to locate the port so the results of the bombing were uncertain. Lewin was not in a good vein of luck as he was involved in a flying accident three days later during a training flight. While landing on the secondary runway at Middleton St. George, the aircraft (L9514) veered to the right and the starboard undercarriage collapsed when the wheel dug into the soft ground. The aircraft was declared damaged beyond economical repair and was converted to an instructional airframe. The following night, three Halifaxes took off just before midnight to attack Cologne but S/L Bickford's aircraft (L9523) had to return early due to a faulty hatch. The other two aircraft (Sgt McHale/L9518 and Sgt McDonald/L9516) completed the raid without incident and had returned by 5.30 in the morning. The next raid carried out on 20/21 June - Kiel - was uneventful despite the heavy flak encountered. Four Halifaxes were detailed again against Kiel three nights later but this time one failed to return. P/O W.K. Stobbs and his crew (L9492) were shot down by *Oblt* Reinhold Eckardt of II./NJG 1. All but one crewman perished with Sgt J.S. Lipton becoming a PoW. It was the first operational loss for 76. The squadron participated in two more raids in the month (26/27th with one aircraft and 29/30th with two aircraft) but with no further loss.

July was the first full month of operations for the squadron but, compared to 35 Sqn, 76 completed a third less while participating in the same number of raids (nine). The first three raids (2/3 July – Bremen, 5/6 July – Magdeburg, 7/8 July – Frankfurt) were uneventful and all aircraft returned to base safely despite heavy flak sometimes being encountered. However, flak was more accurate on the following raid (8/9 July – Leuna) and three of the seven aircraft despatched were damaged to various degrees and two airmen of L9528 were wounded by shrapnel (the flight engineer, Sgt Kenworthy, and the pilot, S/L Bickford). The other Halifaxes damaged were L9496, flown by Sgt Smith, and L9517 (F/O McKenna). All aircraft returned safely from the next three raids (14/15 July and 19/20 July – Hannover, 21/22 July – Mannheim), but this wasn't the case for the day raid in which the squadron participated on the 24th (see above - the attack on La Pallice where the German battleships were moored). Two Halifaxes were shot down by Bf109s. The entire S/L Williams crew of L9494 were taken prisoners, four crewmen of L3529, including the captain (F/L Lewin formerly of 35 Sqn) were killed while the other three became PoWs. A third Halifax (L9517), and her entire crew, was lost to flak. In return, one Bf109 each was claimed as destroyed by the gunners of L9496 (W/C Jarman) and L9531 (Sgt Drummond). For this action the Wing Commander was awarded an immediate DSO (he added to his DFC received two weeks previously) and an immediate DFC was awarded to F/O G.M. Brisbane while Sgt G.A. Fraser received the DFM. The loss of the three Halifaxes was a severe blow for the squadron and it did not return to operations until the 30th. That night, three aircraft were sent to Cologne and, happily, all returned to base safely.

Berlin and Karlsruhe were attacked during the first week of August. L9516 failed to return from the latter. One crewmember was killed and the six survivors became prisoners. One of them, F/L T.B. Leigh, an Australian serving with the RAF, was later executed by the Gestapo in March 1944 for taking part in The Great Escape. The squadron was again badly hit on the night of 12/13 August when it lost another three Halifaxes during a raid on Berlin. Fourteen men perished and seven, including F/L Christopher C. Cheshire (the brother of Leonard Cheshire who would later command the squadron), were made PoWs. His aircraft was shot down by flak while L9531 (Sgt Whitfield) was shot down by a night fighter (claimed by *Ltn* Hans Autenrieth of 6./NJG 1). Halifax L9562 stalled during its approach to base and burst into flames on impact. August was not over for the crews and more losses were to come even though the next raids were free of any incident. On the raid of 29/30 August to Frankfurt, L9518 crashed on return to base due to a shortage of petrol. The captain, S/L Bickford, ordered the crew to bale out, which they all did, but the parachute of Sgt Duckmanton opened too late and S/L Bickford was killed too while jumping out of the aircraft (thought to have jumped too late). On the last day of August, S/L Sutton (who gained a DFC with No. 58 Squadron) was posted from No. 4 Group to take command of the squadron the following day. More changes occurred regarding the leadership in September. The Flight Commanders also changed with S/L J.T. Bouwens (from 51 Sqn) taking over B Flight and F/L Hillary assuming command of A Flight. Generally speaking, after the heavy losses of August, the squadron's participation in the raids over Continental Europe was reduced and only about a dozen sorties were recorded for the month. That didn't prevent losses, however, as one Halifax crashed (L9567/M – P/O R.E. Hutchin) one hour and 10 minutes after take off for Brest. Hutchin was killed in the crash. More than 20 sorties were carried out in October. Brest, Nuremberg, Bremen, Wilhelmshaven, Mannheim, Emden and Cherbourg and Dunkirk were bombed but only one Halifax (L9602/N – F/Sgt C.S. O'Brien RCAF), and her entire crew, were lost (over Dunkirk). The only other event worthy of note in October was the allocation, on the 24th, of the first Mk II to the squadron, (L9611).

In November, the number of sorties was reduced due to the bad weather and the raid over Berlin, launched by five Mk Is and one Mk II on the night of 7/8 November, was conducted in very difficult conditions but all aircraft returned safely to base. Three more raids (on the 9th, 25th and 30th) were carried out and involved nine Halifaxes (including four Mk IIs) but the aircraft all returned safely to base. These last three raids of the month were carried out early in the evening and the crews were able to return to base before midnight. In December, more changes occurred. A new commander, W/C Young from No. 77 Sqn, and more Mk IIs were taken on charge and indicated a new era for the squadron. That month the squadron was flying Mk IIs only on operations while maintaining some Mk Is as immediate reserves. That is why the Mk I continued to fly some ops (to replace an unserviceable Mk II at the last moment). That is what happened for the day raid on Brest on 30 December. Sgt Morin took off in L9383/M after his Mk II encountered a technical problem. This situation continued until February when the last such sortie was carried out by a Mk I (the squadron soon had enough Mk IIs on hand to fulfil its operational needs). A last loss on 30 January was recorded on return from Trondheim in Norway where L9581 was obliged to dicth off the Sctottish coast, (crew safe) the last sortie recorded for a Halifax Mk I with an operational squadron took place on 13 February 1942 when L9601 took off at 02.27, for Cologne, and returned to base at 08.54. The crew was captained by Sgt Lambeth. It was now the role of the successor of the Mk I to continue the bombing campaign of Continental Europe.

A moment of deep concentration. Aircrew of 76 Sqn preparing their equipment before their next night over occupied Europe. At the time, Bomber Command squadrons were suffering heavy losses and the chances of a crew completing a tour safely were not very high.

A view of L9530 which was allocated to 76 Sqn on 06.06.41. It failed to return from a raid to Berlin two months later, crashing 40 km NE of Bremen, manned by F/L Christopher Cheshire and crew. Two were killed and five, including Cheshire, became prisoners. Christopher Cheshire was the brother of Leonard Cheshire.

Summary of the aircraft lost on Operations - 76 Squadron

T/O Date	Pilot	S/N	Origin	Serial	Code	Fate
23.06.41	P/O Walter K. Stobbs	RAF No. 86396	RAF	L9492		†
	Sgt Alan Turner	RAF No. 570035	RAF			†
	Sgt Jack L. Cullum	RAF No. 748640	RAF			†
	F/Sgt George H. Barnard	RAF No. 939872	RAF			†
	Sgt John S. Lipton	RAF No. 976655	RAF			PoW
	Sgt Robert S. Adair	RAF No. 980197	RAF			†
24.07.41	S/L Walter R. Williams	RAF No. 39359	RAF	L9494		PoW
	P/O John G. Ireton	RAF No. 89842	RAF			PoW
	Sgt Alexander H.J. Turner	RAF No. 567326	RAF			PoW
	Sgt Leonard J. Butler	RAF No. 944660	RAF			PoW
	Sgt Norman Kershaw	RAF No. 619641	RAF			PoW
	Sgt Samuel Jones	RAF No. 984206	RAF			PoW
	Sgt George R. Wedderburn	RAF No. 909574	RAF			PoW
	P/O Joseph F.P.J. McKenna	RAF No. 84935	RAF	L9517		†
	Sgt Roger F.S. Ford-Hutchinson	RAF No. 1101878	RAF			†
	Sgt George Summers	RAF No. 967240	RAF			†
	Sgt Valentine A. Davis	RAF No. 939726	RAF			†
	Sgt John M. Pilbeam	RAF No. 918421	RAF			†
	Sgt Leonard T. Rice	RAF No. 518719	RAF			†
	F/Sgt Roy W.J. Hill	RAF No. 551932	RAF			†
	F/L Austin E. Lewin	RAF No. 84304	RAF	L9529		†
	Sgt William H.J. Gourley	Aus.402118	RAAF			†
	F/Sgt Charles H. Horner	RAF No. 560615	RAF			†
	Sgt Benjamin Philipps	RAF No. 974527	RAF			PoW
	Sgt Percy J. Vickery	RAF No. 981272	RAF			†
	Sgt William A. Finlayson	RAF No. 565372	RAF			PoW
	F/O Norman W. McLeod	RAF No. 42259	RAF			PoW
05.08.41	Sgt Thomas A. Byrne	RAF No. 748546	RAF	L9516		PoW
	Sgt Cyril B. Flockhart	RAF No. 628366	RAF			PoW
	Sgt John H. Pitt	RAF No. 645871	RAF			PoW
	Sgt Leonard A. Thompson	RAF No. 968105	RAF			PoW
	Sgt George W.S. Taylor	RAF No. 940022	RAF			PoW
	Sgt Robert Brown	RAF No. 952523	RAF			†
	F/L Thomas B. Leigh	RAF No. 46462	(AUS)/RAF			PoW
12.08.41	F/L Christopher C. Cheshire	RAF No. 87635	RAF	L9530	MP-L	PoW
	Sgt Paul H.T. Horrox	RAF No. 1002387	RAF			PoW
	Sgt Reginald C. Wash	RAF No. 623625	RAF			PoW
	F/Sgt Gordon J. Smalley	RAF No. 754689	RAF			PoW
	Sgt Edward C. Gurmin	RAF No. 972802	RAF			PoW
	Sgt Alexnander T. Niven	RAF No. 1325203	RAF			†
	F/Sgt William Woods	RAF No. 531299	(IRE)/RAF			†
	Sgt Clarence E. Whitfield	RAF No. 923812	RAF	L9531		†
	Sgt John J. Berry	RAF No. 1166613	RAF			†
	Sgt Kenneth R.F. Kenworthy	RAF No. 569378	RAF			PoW
	P/O Victor D. Durham	RAF No. 64280	RAF			†
	Sgt Alfred Critchlow	RAF No. 978005	RAF			†
	Sgt Norman F. Brotherton	RAF No. 956849	RAF			†
	F/Sgt William A.I. Bone	RAF No. 581434	RAF			PoW
	Sgt John McHale	RAF No. 741064	RAF	L9562		†
	Sgt Reginald J. McInnes	Can./ R.60280	RCAF			†
	Sgt Cecil Austin	RAF No. 565799	RAF			†
	Sgt Stanley C. Mayes	RAF No. 755992	RAF			†

T/O Date	Pilot (and crew when available)	S/N	Origin	Serial	Code	Fate
	Sgt Edward P. Hogan	RAF No. 940001	RAF			†
	Sgt Lorne E. Brown	Can./ R.64143	RCAF			†
	F/Sgt James G.S. West	RAF No. 517461	RAF			†
29.08.41	S/L Richard Bickford	RAF No. 37462	RAF	L9518		†
	P/O Philip H.T. Jones	RAF No. 87362	RAF			-
	Cpl Peter D. Randall	RAF No. 567345	RAF			-
	F/Sgt James Flannigan	RAF No. 759151				-
	Sgt John J. O'Reilly	RAF No. 939114	RAF			-
	Sgt George W. Duckmanton	RAF No. 904067	RAF			†
14.09.41	P/O Ronald E. Hutchin	RAF No. 104449	RAF	L9567		†
	Sgt Charles E. Wood	RAF No. 568343	RAF			-
	Sgt Crowe	?	?			-
	Sgt Browne	?	?			-
	F/Sgt James Flannigan	RAF No. 759151	RAF			-
	Sgt Reginald Littlehales	RAF No. 1268196	RAF			-
	Sgt Wallace	?	?			-
12.10.41	F/Sgt Elmer B. Muttart	Can./ R.64729	RCAF	L9561		†
	P/O Norman F. Trayler	RAF No. 101563	RAF			PoW
	Sgt David Cotsell	RAF No. 567496	RAF			PoW
	Sgt Leslie A. Roberts	RAF No. 565746	RAF			PoW
	Sgt Reginald W.P. Alexander	RAF No. 748073	RAF			PoW
	Sgt William H. Hunt	RAF No. 910914	RAF			PoW
	Sgt George H. Patterson	RAF No. 943602	RAF			PoW
	Sgt John W. Duffield	RAF No. 923202	RAF			PoW
31.10.41	F/Sgt Charles S. O'Brien	Can./ R.65254	RCAF	L9602	MP-N	†
	P/O Neil F. McLean	NZ403876	RNZAF			†
	Sgt Charles E. Wood	RAF No. 568343	RAF			†
	Sgt John R. Johnson	Can./ R.56089	RCAF			†
	F/Sgt James Flannigan	RAF No. 759151	RAF			†
	P/O Francis C. Brooks	Can./ J.15849	RCAF			†
	Sgt James Mycock	RAF No. 1378898	RAF			†
29.01.42	Sgt John W.H. Harwood	RAF No. 1152316	RAF	L9581	MP-Q	-
	Sgt DonaldM. Smardon	Can./ R.77069	RCAF			-
	Sgt Patey	?	?			-
	Sgt Young	?	?			-
	Sgt Scott	?	?			-
	Sgt Roche	?	?			-
	Sgt Petch	?	?			-

Total: 13

Summary of the aircraft lost on Operations - 76 Squadron

T/O Date	Pilot (and crew when available)	S/N	Origin	Serial	Code	Fate
15.06.41	P/O Austin E. Lewin	RAF No. 84304	RAF	L9514		-
21.07.41	P/O Leonard R. Blackwell	RAF No. 100610	RAF	L9533		†
	Sgt Kenneth N. Hudgell	RAF No. 964546	RAF			†
	Sgt Alfred J. Grenyer	RAF No. 568042	RAF			†
	Sgt John W.R. Boggis	RAF No. 905397	RAF			†
	Sgt Albert J. Howes	RAF No. 920805	RAF			†
15.01.42	Sgt James B. Stark	RAF No. 1051848	RAF	L9578	MP-C	-
06.02.42	Sgt Hewart J. Lambeth	RAF No. 1255089	RAF	L9570	MP-E	-

Total: 4

Claims - 76 Squadron (Confirmed and Probable)

Date	Capt of the crew	SN	Origin	Type	Serial	Code	Nb	Cat.
24.07.41	W/C Geoffrey T. **Jarman**	RAF No. 29211	RAF	Bf109	**L9496**		1.0	C
	Sgt Henry H. **Drummond**	RAF No. 968515	RAF	Bf109	**L9531**		1.0	C
		Total: 2.0						

SECOND-LINE UNITS AND END OF SERVICE LIFE

The introduction of four-engine bombers into RAF service produced several difficulties, among them flying training. All of the pilots graduated from twin-engine aircraft in OTUs (Operational Training Unit) and, initially, 35 Squadron carried out its own early conversion training. However, it soon became clear that this measure was only a stop-gap and something more adequate had to be found. The problem was similar for the new Stirling squadrons.

The first step was to form Conversion Flights (CF) for training crews to handle the new heavy bombers and complete the training undertaken on Wellingtons or Whitleys. As far as the Halifax was concerned, the first Conversion Flight to be formed was No. 28 in August 1941. At first partly an experiment, it was formalised on 4 November with a normal allocation of eight Halifaxes. Its aircraft included six drawn from Nos. 35 and 76 Sqns but total numbers remained small in the four months of existence of the flight with only 12 in all, including the prototype L7245, issued to boost numbers. Indeed, the front line units still had priority and, considering the operational losses, few Halifax Mk Is were made available for the CFs.

Indeed, in December 1941, it was decided to expand the process by establishing a new training syllabus consisting of one Heavy Conversion Unit (HCU) per Group plus one Conversion Flight of four aircraft per squadron. While No.28 CF was eventually absorbed into No. 1652 HCU on 2 January 1942, No. 102 CF was formed during January 1942 using five Mk.Is and was followed by Nos. 35 - two Mk.Is - and 76 CF - two aircraft also - the following month, No. 78 CF in March (three Mk Is in the inventory). One more Mk I CF was formed at that time, No. 10, but did not receive any Mk Is. From there on, as each new Halifax Squadron formed in 1942, it established its own CF but, as far as the Mk I was concerned, only the Canadian No. 408 CF was allocated two Mk Is, L9524 and L9532, after the initial Conversion Flights. This structure lasted until 7 October 1942 when all of the CFs were disbanded and absorbed by the HCUs. Seven Mk Is were wrecked or damaged beyond economical repair during that time, including three from 102 CF and one from 28 CF (which caused the death of eight crewmen). It is worth noting, however, that this accident did not occur during a training flight but on a transit flight to the Handley Page facility at Radlett. Taking off at 10.25 from Leconfield, the weather was very bad and the aircraft hit a hill at Knipton, near Grantham, giving no chance of survival for the men on board who included one DFC recipient (F/L Owen, the captain) and two DFM awardees (F/O Gibb and Sgt Mayston).

Of the new HCUs formed in January 1942, No. 1652 would remain the main operator of the Halifax Mk I over the next few months but some Mk Is found their way to No. 1658 HCU and No. 1659 HCU (RCAF) when they were formed in October 1942 as the Canadian conversion unit for the Halifaxes. The training programme allowed for about 20 hours of instruction and covered all essential aspects:

Familiarisation flight: 0.5 hour (1 flight)
Dual circuits and landings: 3.0 hours (3-4 flights)
Solo circuits and landings: 0.5 hour (1 flight)
Dual check and overshoot: 0.5 hour (1 flight)
Solo dual check and three-engine handling: 2.0 hours (2 flights)
Solo flight: 1.0 hour (1 flight)
Dual check and two-engine handling: 1.0 hour (1 flight)
Solo climb to 12,000 feet and bomb door operation: 1.5 hours (1 flight)
Dual, draining fuel tanks and mid-air changeover: 1.0 hour (1 flight)
Solo dual instrument flying: 3.0 hours (3 flights)
Dual, take-off with full bomb load, cross-country, and tank changeover: 2.0 hours (1 flight)
Dual check including three-engine overshoot and landing: 1.0 hour (1 flight)

Once this course was completed the pilots were posted to a squadron, where the CF would provide the final training with the rest of the crew, but this system was flexible depending on whether the pilot was experienced or not. A number of Halifax Mk I accidents were recorded with the first being as early as 6 January 1942 (four days after the formation of the HCU). Eleven more followed in the next 18 months and took the lives of sixteen airmen. As with other types, the Halifaxes were also called upon to reinforce the Bomber Command fleet for operational missions and a couple of sorties were carried out during that period including involvement in the 1,000 bomber raid of 31 May 1942. One aircraft, L9605, was lost to an enemy night fighter (possibly Oblt Reinhard Knacke of 3./NJG 1) while heading to Koln. With one killed and three PoWs. Among the latter, W/O Lowman would be killed on 19 April 1945 in a tragic attack by Typhoons on a prisoner of war column near Grese. In all, about 20 Halifax Mk Is were used by No. 1652 HCU, five by No. 1658 and one each by Nos. 1659, 1662 and 1663.

By mid-1943, the few Halifax Mk Is still flying were weary and, as the number of subsequent marks became increasingly available, the aircraft were progressively withdrawn from use. Many were converted to instructional airframes, a very useful task, from Spring 1942 but the conversion reached its peak the following Autumn and no less than 20 Mk Is (of the 86 built) eventually ended their career as such. By that time the Halifax had become a major component of the Bomber Command with the Mk III about to enter service.

By mid-1943, the Halifax Mk Is still flying were weary and, as the number of subsequent marks became increasingly available, the aircraft were progressively withdrawn from use. Many were converted to instructional airframes, a very useful task, from Spring 1942 but the conversion reached its peak the following Autumn and no less than 20 Mk Is (of the 86 built) eventually ended their career as such. By that time the Halifax had become a major component of the Bomber Command with the Mk III about to enter service.

Summary of the aircraft lost on Operations - Training Units

Date	Pilot	S/N	Origin	Serial	Code	Unit	Fate
31.05.42	F/L Stanley G. **Wright**	RAF No. 60115	RAF	**L9605**	GV-Y	1652 CU	**PoW**
	W/O Hugh P. **Lowan**	RAF No. 570626	RAF				**PoW**
	F/L Douglas G. **Cookson**	NZ404532	RNZAF				**PoW**
	W/O Ronald J. **Tavener**	RAF No. 964024	RAF				**PoW**
	Sgt Kenneth J.A. **Manley**	RAF No. 951350	RAF				†

Total: 1

Halifax MK. I, L9509, coded C and serving with No. 1652 HCU at Marston Moor, taken while undergoing an inspection in mid-1942. L9509 was allocated to this unit in April 1942 and served with it until being victim of a flying accident in April 1943. (*E. Marsden*)

Summary of the aircraft lost on Operations - Training Units

Date	Pilot and crew when known	S/N	Origin	Serial	Code	Unit	Fate
22.12.41	F/L Robert F. Owen	RAF No. 84914	RAF	**L9522**		28 CF	†
	P/O Richard P.W. Barker	NZ41464	RNZAF				†
	P/O William S. Beattie	NZ41301	RNZAF				†
	Sgt Leslie Merrifield	RAF No. 702345	RAF				†
	F/O Eric A.F. Gibb	RAF No. 104430	RAF				†
	Sgt Stanley R. Mayston	RAF No. 908800	RAF				†
	Sgt James A. Denning	RAF No. 939302	RAF				†
	Cpl James A. Hancock	RAF No. 648598	RAF				†
06.01.42	F/O Peter Johnston	RAF No. 68139	RAF	**L9519**		1652 CU	-
13.03.42	W/C James B. Tait	RAF No. 33291	RAF	**L9513**		1652 CU	-
	S/L Albert J.D. Snow	RAF No. 41076	RAF				-
14.04.42	F/O Frederick J. Joshua	RAF No. 87041	RAF	**L9576**	E	1652 CU	†
	F/Sgt David R. Cox	Can./ R.65319	RCAF				†
	Sgt Alfred T. Howell	RAF No. 1380271	RAF				†
	Sgt James E. Gurney	RAF No. 527385	RAF				†
	Sgt Ernest J. Spencer	RAF No. 903905	RAF				†
	Sgt Gilbert Marks	RAF No. 1169564	RAF				†
	AC1 Colin G.C. Keighley*	RAF No. 1333962	RAF				†
	AC1 Thomas Mahady*	RAF No. 1371443	RAF				†
	AC2 Frederick S. Goodwin*	RAF No. 1499120	RAF				†
07.05.42	-**	-		**L9568**		35 CF	-
08.05.42	P/O Charles Mitchener	RAF No. 102558	RAF	**L9583**		78 CF	-
	Sgt Stevens	?	?				-
16.08.42	Sgt William Beck	RAF No. 1376637	RAF	**L9496**		1652 CU	-
23.08.42	F/L Robert J. Neal	RAF No. 36258	RAF	**L9601**		78 CF	-
09.10.42	P/O Francis Leach	RAF No. 113402	RAF	**L9574**		1658 CU	†
	Sgt Geoffrey E. Broughton	RAF No. 1311939	RAF				†
	Sgt Alexander H. Isaac	RAF No. 1190773	RAF				†
	Sgt George Bukcland	RAF No. 1320255	RAF				†
18.10.42	Sgt Anthony J. Grant	RAF No. 1337376	RAF	**L9510**		102 CF	-
31.10.42	Sgt William S. Allard	RAF No. 1270886	RAF	**L9491**	Q	1652 CU	Inj.
	LAC David P. Macdonald	RAF No. 1020935	RAF				Inj.
	Sgt Frederick B. Ward	RAF No. 1381481	RAF				-
	Sgt Jospeh W. Young	RAF No. 1216336	RAF				-
02.11.42	Sgt Simon W. Templar	RAF No. 1330718	RAF	**L9565**		102 CF	-
	Sgt Frederick D. Buchwalter	RAF No. 1330634	RAF				-
03.11.42	Sgt Peter A. Grant	RAF No. 1337376	RAF	**L9584**		102 CF	-
29.11.42	F/Sgt John D.W. Stenhouse	RAF No. 1268035	RAF	**L9608**		1652 CU	-
04.01.43	F/L Sydney J.B. Hamilton	RAF No. 62703	RAF	**L9569**		1658 CU	-
	Sgt M.C. Smith	RAF No.696994	RAF				-
03.04.43	F/Sgt Alexander McA. Sargent	RAF No. 937481	RAF	**L9509**		1652 CU	-
14.04.43	Sgt Desmond E.A. Lander	RAF No. 1333728	RAF	**L9525**		1652 CU	-
25.05.43	F/O Alastair I.T. Moir	RAF No. 137208	RAF	**L9571**	H	1652 CU	†
	F/Sgt Daniel E. Veness	Aus.411620	RAAF				†
	Sgt Frederick W. Barns	RAF No. 927683	RAF				†
	Sgt T.F. King	?	?				-
	Sgt J. Winchester	?	?				-
23.06.43	P/O Henry D. Alcock	NZ403928	RNZAF	**L9575**		1652 CU	-
	Sgt Douglas A. Robinson	RAF No. 1215638	RAF				-

*Passenger

**Ground accident, hit by Halifax II W1051.

Total: 19

THE REGISTER

Serial	TOC	Unit	From	To	Code	Fate	Nb of sorties
L7244	25.11.39	A&AEE	24.09.40	23.1140			
		35 Sqn	23.11.40	03.08.41			
		AFEE	15.03.42	11.08.42		To 3299M 11.08.42	
L7245	07.09.40	A&AEE	11.09.40	05.11.41			
		28 CF	07.12.41	24.02.42		To 3474M 24.12.42	
L9485	06.08.40	A&AEE	26.04.41	08.07.42		To 3362M 15.09.42	

L9485, the first production aircraft was retained by the A&AEE to conduct various experiments.

Serial	TOC	Unit	From	To	Code	Fate	Nb of sorties
L9486	30.08.40	A&AEE	30.08.40	17.10.40			
		35 Sqn	10.12.40	12.11.41	TL-B		2
					TL-G		4
		28 CF	12.11.41	02.01.42			
		1652 CU	03.03.42	14.04.42		To 3005M 14.04.42	
L9487	29.10.40	35 Sqn	04.01.41	13.01.41		FA 13.01.41	
L9488	29.09.40	35 Sqn	16.02.41	10.06.41	TL-M		2
		76 Sqn	10.06.41	02.08.41	?		2
		RAE	29.08.42	24.04.43		To 3678M 24.04.43	
L9489	20.10.40	35 Sqn	12.01.41	10.03.41	TL-F	SD 10.03.41/Le Havre	1
L9490	24.10.40	35 Sqn	16.02.41	17.07.41	TL-L	FA 17.07.41	3
L9491	28.10.40	35 Sqn	23.03.41	28.10.41	TL-J		5
		28 CF	28.10.41	02.01.42			
		1652 CU	02.01.42	31.10.42		FA 31.10.42	
L9492	24.11.40	35 Sqn	01.03.41	19.06.41	TL-K		4
		76 Sqn	19.06.41	24.06.41	?	FTR 24.06.41/Kiel	1
L9493	24.11.40	35 Sqn	01.02.41	16.04.41	TL-G	FA 16.04.41	2
L9494	11.12.40	35 Sqn	28.02.41	20.06.41	?		-
		76 Sqn	20.06.41	24.07.41	?	FTR 24.07.41/La Palice	2
L9495	11.12.40	35 Sqn	16.03.41	17.07.41	TL-B	FA 17.07.41	8
L9496	22.12.40	35 Sqn	15.02.41	19.06.41	TL-B		6
		76 Sqn	19.06.41	28.10.41	?		5
		28 CF	28.10.41	02.01.42			
		1652 CU	02.01.42	16.08.42		FA 16.08.42	
L9497	22.12.40	35 Sqn	19.07.41	13.08.41	TL-K	Crashed/Berlin	1
L9498	22.12.40	35 Sqn	21.02.41	13.06.41	TL-T	FA 13.06.41	3
L9499	22.12.40	35 Sqn	03.0341	30.06.41	TL-Q	FTR 30.06.41/Kiel	5
L9500	01.01.41	35 Sqn	12.03.41	14.08.41	TL-Z		1
					TL-H	FTR 14.08.41/Magdeburg	17
L9501	01.01.41	35 Sqn	18.03.41	29.08.41	TL-Y	FTR Duisburg	14
L9502	24.01.41	35 Sqn	25.02.41	08.07.41	TL-R	FTR Frankfurt	4
L9503	02.02.41	35 Sqn	23.02.41	16.09.41	TL-P	FTR Hamburg	20
L9504	02.02.41	35 Sqn	10.03.41	21.02.42	TL-H		19
		102 CF	21.02.42	14.01.43			
		1652 CU	14.01.43	15.03.43		To 3506M 15.03.43	

Halifax Mk I L9485 in flight while conducting trials with Boulton Paul C Mk V mid-upper and ventral K turrets Damaged in early July 1942, it was returned to Handley Page on 8 July for conversion into Instructional Airframe and was issued to No. 4 School of Technical training on the following 15 September.

L9505	02.02.41	RAE	15.11.41	05.09.42			To 3677M 15.05.43	
L9506	02.02.41	35 Sqn	04.04.41	16.06.41	TL-X		Crashed/Hannover	3
L9507	02.02.41	35 Sqn	31.03.41	26.07.41	TL-W		FTR Berlin	10
L9508	28.02.41	35 Sqn	06.04.41	03.09.41	TL-F			11
					TL-X		FTR Berlin	11
L9509	28.02.41	35 Sqn	06.04.41	13.08.41	TL-C			4
		HCF	28.10.41	07.11.41				
		35 Sqn	07.11.41	20.11.41				
		28 CF	20.11.41	07.04.42				
		1652 CU	07.04.42	03.04.43	C		FA 03.04.43	
L9510	28.02.41	35 Sqn	23.04.41	12.05.41	?			-
		76 Sqn	12.05.41	20.07.41	?			4
			30.06.42	02.07.42				
		102 CF	02.07.42	18.10.42			FA 18.10.42	
L9511	28.02.41	35 Sqn	10.05.41	11.06.42	TL-D			10
					TL-P			2
		1652 CU	15.06.42	06.43	Y		To 3761M June 43	1
L9512	28.02.41	35 Sqn	02.06.41	24.07.41	TL-U		FTR La Palice	4
L9513	08.03.41	35 Sqn	31.03.41	05.05.41	?			1
		76 Sqn	05.05.41	28.10.41	?			4
		28 CF	28.10.41	02.01.42				
		1652 CU	02.01.42	13.03.42			FA 13.03.42	
L9514	15.03.41	35 Sqn	10.04.41	25.05.41	?		FA 15.06.41 to 3506M	-
		76 Sqn	25.05.41	15.06.41	?			1

Copy of the movement card of Halifax L9515, showing clearly its mark, (II) and engines installed (Merlin XXs).

L9516	15.03.41	35 Sqn	15.04.41	03.05.41	?			-
		76 Sqn	03.05.41	06.08.41	?		FTR Karlsruhe	12
L9517	15.03.41	35 Sqn	23.04.41	12.05.41	?			-
		76 Sqn	12.05.41	24.07.41	?		FTR La Palice (TT:112.8)	10
L9518	15.03.41	35 Sqn	20.04.41	05.05.41	?			-
		76 Sqn	05.05.41	30.08.41	?		Crashed/Frakfurt (TT:83.2)	5
L9519	15.03.41	35 Sqn	28.04.41	05.05.41	?			
		76 Sqn	08.05.41	?				
		1652 CU	?	06.01.42			FA 06.01.42	
L9520	15.03.41	A&AEE	09.12.41	16.12.41				
		CRD	16.12.41	17.08.43			To 3676M 17.08.43	
L9521	26.04.41	35 Sqn	02.05.41	09.07.41	TL-Z		FTR Leuna	3

Serial	Date	Unit	From	To	Code	Fate	Ops
L9522	26.04.41	35 Sqn	03.05.41	09.11.41			
		28 CF	09.11.41	22.12.41		FA 22.12.41	
L9523	26.04.41	35 Sqn	06.05.41	12.05.41	?		-
		76 Sqn	12.05.41	13.06.42	?		8
					MP-Y		7
		76 CF	30.06.42	13.07.42			
		78 CF	13.07.42	11.05.43		To 3690M 11.05.43	
L9524	26.04.41	35 Sqn	26.05.41	14.02.42	TL-V		10
		10 CF	14.02.42	12.10.42			
		1659 CU	12.10.42	13.10.42			
		408 CF	13.10.42	?		To 3489M *(date not recorded)*	
L9525	26.04.41	35 Sqn	28.05.41	28.10.41			-
		28 CF	28.10.41	02.01.42			
		1652 CU	02.01.42	26.03.43	W		4
		1663 CU	26.03.43	14.04.43		FA 14.04.43 (TT:493.9)	
L9526	26.04.41	35 Sqn	22.05.41	11.09.41	TL-O	Crashed/Turin	9
L9527	26.04.41	35 Sqn	27.05.41	24.07.41	TL-M	FTR La Palice	4
L9528	26.04.41	35 Sqn	02.06.41	06.06.41	?		-
		76 Sqn	06.06.41	06.06.42	?		1
					MP-P		2
		76 CF	06.06.42	31.08.42			
		1658 CU	31.08.42	04.10.42			
		76 CF	01.12.42	27.06.43		To 3882M 27.06.43	
L9529	26.04.41	35 Sqn	02.06.41	06.06.41	?		-
		76 Sqn	06.06.41	24.07.41	?	FTR La Palice (TT:53.9)	7
L9530	26.04.41	35 Sqn	04.06.41	06.06.41	?		-
		76 Sqn	06.06.41	15.08.41	?	FTR Magdeburg	5
L9531	26.04.41	76 Sqn	07.06.41	13.08.41	?	FTR Berlin	2
L9532	26.04.41	76 Sqn	12.06.41	16.01.42	?		1
		1652 CU	16.01.42	17.09.41			
		102 Sqn	17.09.42	08.10.42			
		408 CF	08.10.42	21.12.42			
		1659 CU	21.12.42	08.07.43		To 3953M 27.06.43	
L9533	26.04.41	76 Sqn	14.06.41	21.07.41		FA 21.07.41 (TT: 6.9)	
L9534	26.04.41	76 Sqn	15.06.41	02.11.41	MP-T		9
		28 CF	02.11.41	02.01.42			
		1652 CU	02.01.42	05.01.43			
		1659 CU	05.01.43	?		To 3455M *(date not recorded)*	
L9560	?	35 Sqn	25.06.41	03.09.41	TL-F	FTR Berlin	10
L9561	12.06.41	76 Sqn	30.06.41	13.10.41	MP-E	FTR Nurnberg (TT:99.7)	9
					MP-H		3
L9562	12.06.41	76 Sqn	07.07.41	13.08.41	?	Crashed/Berlin	3
L9563	?	76 Sqn	28.06.41	17.06.42	?		1
					MP-U		3
		78 CF	17.06.42	31.12.42			
		1658 CU	31.12.42	11.05.43		To 3691M 11.05.43	
L9564	12.06.41	76 Sqn	02.08.41	18.11.41	MP-A		5
		28 CF	18.11.41	02.01.42			
		1652 CU	02.01.42	22.06.43	Q	To 3850M 22.05.43	2
L9565	12.06.41	76 Sqn	02.08.41	28.10.41	MP-B		7
		28 CF	28.10.41	02.01.42			
		1652 CU	02.01.42	09.05.42			
		102 CF	09.05.42	02.11.42		FA 02.11.42 (TT:431.9)	
L9566	?	35 Sqn	22.06.41	11.09.41	TL-R	FTR Turin	9
L9567	12.06.41	76 Sqn	27.08.41	14.09.41	MP-N	Crashed/Brest (TT: 8.5)	1
L9568	17.06.41	35 Sqn	09.09.41	11.01.42	TL-J		10
		35 CF	11.01.42	07.05.42		Ac.07.05.42	
L9569	20.06.41	35 Sqn	02.08.41	14.02.42	TL-K		15
		10 CF	14.02.42	07.07.42			
		1658 CU	?	05.01.43		Ac04.01.43 (TT:336.2)	
L9570	12.06.41	76 Sqn	10.10.41	06.02.42	MP-E	Ac.06.02.42	2
L9571	12.06.41	35 Sqn	01.10.41	11.01.42	TL-C		2
		35 CF	11.01.42	31.12.42	GV-Y		
		1652 CU	31.12.42	25.05.43		Ac.25.05.43 (TT:343.9)	
L9572	12.06.41	35 Sqn	30.07.41	25.08.41	TL-G	FTR Dusseldorf	5
L9573	?	76 Sqn	12.08.41	16.03.42	MP-D		1

Serial	Date	Unit	From	To	Code	Fate	Ops
		76 CF	20.06.42	31.12.42			
		1658 CU	31.12.42	29.06.43		To 3865M 29.06.43	
L9574	11.07.41	76 Sqn	16.08.41	30.06.42	MP-R		3
		76 CF	30.06.42	?			
		1658 CU	?	09.10.42		Ac.09.10.42 (TT:199.6)	
L9575	11.07.41	35 Sqn	20.10.41	11.01.42	TL-F		1
		35 CF	11.01.42	31.12.42	GV-W		
		1652 CU	31.12.42	23.06.43		Ac.23.06.43	
L9576	11.07.41	1652 CU	01.04.42	14.04.42	GV-E	Ac.14.04.42	
L9577	?	LPTB	30.06.41	18.03.42			
		EEC	18.03.42	13.05.42			
		76 CF	26.06.42	?			
		1658 CU	?	02.02.43			
		1662 CU	01.01.44	25.03.44*		Ac.25.03.44	
L9578	11.07.41	76 Sqn	29.08.41	15.01.42	MP-C	Ac.15.01.42	2
L9579	11.07.41	35 Sqn	26.09.41	13.10.41	TL-P	Crashed (TT:23.9)	2
L9580	11.07.41	35 Sqn	03.10.41	02.11.41	TL-N		4
		28 CF	02.11.41	02.01.42			
		1652 CU	02.01.42	?	S	To 3454M *(date not recorded)*	4
L9581	11.07.41	76 Sqn	08.11.41	30.01.42		FTR/Tronheim (TT:28.00)	
L9582	11.07.41	35 Sqn	20.10.41	01.12.41	TL-T	FTR/Hamburg (TT:39.00)	4
L9583	11.07.41	76 Sqn	17.10.41	20.02.42	MP-M		8
		78 CF	20.02.42	08.05.42		Ac.08.05.42	
L9584	26.08.41	35 Sqn	26.10.42	21.02.42	TL-L		5
		102 CF	21.02.42	03.11.42		Ac.03.11.42	
L9600	21.08.41	35 Sqn	15.10.41	12.12.41	TL-U	FTR Cologne (TT:46.1)	3
L9601	21.08.41	76 Sqn	27.09.41	20.02.42	MP-F		6
		78 CF	20.02.42	23.08.42		Ac23.08.42	
L9602	21.08.41	76 Sqn	15.10.41	01.11.41	MP-N	FTR Dunkirk	1
L9603	21.08.41	35 Sqn	22.10.41	08.11.41	TL-P	FTR Essen (TT:10.4)	1
L9604	21.08.41	76 Sqn	20.10.41	23.12.42	MP-W	To 3161M 09.06.42	4
L9505	02.09.41	35 Sqn	16.10.41	25.01.42	TL-D		6
		1652 CU	09.03.42	31.05.42	GV-Y	FTR Cologne (TT:166.3)	1
L9506	02.09.41	35 Sqn	24.09.41	07.04.42	TL-R		11
		35 CF	07.04.42	31.12.42	GV-K		
		1652 CU	31.12.42	14.08.43		To 4046M 14.08.43	
L9607	02.09.41	35 Sqn	15.10.41	22.04.42			-
		35 CF	22.04.42	31.12.42	GV-Z		1
		1652 CU	31.12.42	01.07.43		To 3866M 01.07.43	
L9608	02.09.41	76 Sqn	17.10.41	14.02.42	MP-H		2
		1652 CU	14.02.42	29.11.42	H	Ac.29.11.42 (TT:217.8)	1

*Mk II ocnversion in March 43.

Copy of the accident dated 25 March 1944, sustained by Halifax L9577. This Halifax, delivered as a Mk I (Series 2), was later converted to a Mk II with the installation of Merlin XXs instead of the original Xs, as shown on the card. It is an interesting point as normally only the Series 3 Halifax Mk Is had the provision to get equipped with Merlin XX. The exact number of conversions from Mk I to Mk II which took place after the withdrawal of the Mk I from the front line units is not known.

DATE	25.3.44	
SIG.	1652 T.U.	
765(C)	21.4.4	
1669	951.8hr	
412	PR	
FILE	G.67997/14	
CNTY.	Lincs	
A/F	HEMSWELL	

UNIT: 1652 T.U.
A/C TYPE MARK: HALIFAX II
CODE: N
NO.: L9577
DAMAGE: B
COST: 14
ENG. TYPE SINGLE/PORT/O: Merlin XX 245763
PORT/I: Merlin XX 242877
STBD/I: Merlin XX 219994
STBD/O: Merlin XX 236445

FUNCTION	NAME. INITIALS. NATIONALITY	RANK	NUMBER
Pilot	HEWITT (Canadian)	Flt. Lt.	J.10143
Pupil Pilot	Demschuk (Polish)	F/Sgt.	780992

TOTAL TOTAL: 957
TOTAL TYPE: 447
NIGHT TOTAL: 514
NIGHT TYPE: 1
CAS.: 7 / 7

AC: N
FATAL: 7

IN MEMORIAM

Halifax Mk.I

Name	Service No	Rank	Age	Origin	Date	Serial
Adair, Robert Simpson	RAF No.980197	Sgt	n/k	RAF	24.06.41	L9492
Adkins, Arthur Edward Charles	RAF No.101039	P/O	n/k	RAF	29.08.41	L9501
Anderson, James Blain	Can./R.54021	Sgt	n/k	RCAF	25.08.41	L9572
Arnold, Edward Rolfe	RAF No.77908	P/O	25	RAF	10.03.41	L9487
Austin, Cecil	RAF No.565799	Sgt	n/k	RAF	13.08.41	L9562
Barker, Richard Percival William	NZ41464	P/O	25	RAF	22.12.41	L9522
Barnard, George Henry	RAF No.939872	F/Sgt	23	RAF	24.06.41	L9492
Barns, Frederick William	RAF No.927683	F/O	34	RAF	25.05.43	L9571
Bates, Reginald Arthur	RAF No.751214	F/Sgt	n/k	RAF	26.07.41	L9507
Beattie, William Stuart	NZ41301	P/O	24	RAF	22.12.41	L9522
Bell, Ian Redmayne	RAF No.581312	F/Sgt	n/k	RAF	11.12.41	L9600
Berry, John James	RAF No.1166613	Sgt	21	RAF	13.08.41	L9531
Berry, Wallace Llewellyn	Can./R.59127	Sgt	25	RCAF	15.08.41	L9500
Bickford, Richard	RAF No.37462	S/L	30	RAF	30.08.41	L9518
Blackwell, Leonard Richard	RAF No.100610	P/O	26	RAF	21.07.41	L9533
Boggis, John William Rolfe	RAF No.905397	Sgt	24	RAF	21.07.41	L9533
Bolton, Peter George*	RAF No.944667	Sgt	24	RAF	24.07.41	L9524
Brelsford, Harold	RAF No.1162052	P/O	n/k	RAF	29.08.41	L9501
Broadhurst, Stanley	RAF No.550817	Sgt	20	RAF	10.03.41	L9487
Brooks, Francis Conn	Can./J.15849	P/O	25	RCAF	31.10.41	L9602
Brotherton, Norman Frederick	RAF No.956849	Sgt	21	RAF	13.08.41	L9531
Broughton, Geoffrey Eyre	RAF No.1311939	Sgt	21	RAF	09.10.42	L9574
Brown, Harold Stanley	RAF No.108027	P/O	21	RAF	15.09.41	L9503
Brown, Lorne Edwin	Can./R.64143	Sgt	21	RCAF	13.08.41	L9562
Brown, Robert	RAF No.952523	Sgt	n/k	RAF	05.08.41	L9516
Buckland, George	RAF No.1320255	Sgt	19	RAF	09.10.42	L9574
Buckley, Hubert Donald	RAF No.104512	P/O	28	RAF	11.12.41	L9600
Coleman, Noel Eric Henry	RAF No.1107286	Sgt	33	RAF	09.07.41	L9521
Collinge, Robert Victor	RAF No.581204	F/Sgt	22	RAF	26.07.41	L9507
Collins, John	RAF No.905359	F/Sgt	24	RAF	30.11.41	L9582
Collins, Walter Norman	RAF No.617140	Sgt	n/k	RAF	25.08.41	L9572
Cooper, Albert Edward	RAF No.77963	F/O	34	RAF	10.03.41	L9487
Cooper, Ernest Ronald Peter Shackle	RAF No.87050	P/O	26	RAF	26.07.41	L9507
Cox, David Reid	Can./R.65319	F/Sgt	23	RCAF	14.04.42	L9576
Cox, John Alfred Arthur	RAF No.648868	F/Sgt	24	RAF	15.08.41	L9500
Critchlow, Alfred	RAF No.978005	Sgt	n/k	RAF	13.08.41	L9531
Crocker, Frank Wilson	RAF No.911566	Sgt	25	RAF	11.12.41	L9600
Cruickshank, John Milne Rigg	RAF No.1051632	Sgt	23	RAF	26.07.41	L9507
Cullum, Jack Leonard	RAF No.748640	Sgt	n/k	RAF	24.06.41	L9492
Cushion, John Peter Boston	RAF No.88456	P/O	21	RAF	03.09.41	L9560
Davie, Alexander James	RAF No.620056	Sgt	23	RAF	30.06.41	L9499
Davis, Valentine Arthur	RAF No.939726	F/Sgt	21	RAF	24.07.41	L9517
Denning, James Albert	RAF No.939302	Sgt	n/k	RAF	22.12.41	L9522
Duckmanton, George William	RAF No.904067	Sgt	31	RAF	30.08.41	L9518
Dunn, Robert	RAF No.1109715	Sgt	20	RAF	30.06.41	L9499
Durham, Victor Digby	RAF No.64280	P/O	22	RAF	13.08.41	L9531
Esnouf, Greville Gascoyne	RAF No.929408	Sgt	19	RAF	24.07.41	L9527
Flannigan, James	RAF No.759151	F/Sgt	20	RAF	31.10.41	L9602

Ford-Hutchinson, Roger Francis Stuart	RAF No. 84395	Sgt	20	RAF	24.07.41	L9517
Fraser, Douglas Stewart	RAF No. 88869	P/O	19	RAF	03.09.41	L9560
Fuller, Jack	RAF No. 987503	Sgt	21	RAF	25.08.41	L9572
Garner, Michael Gerard	RAF No. 1168520	Sgt	19	RAF	15.08.41	L9500
Gibb, Eric Arthur Fawns	RAF No. 104430	F/O	22	RAF	22.12.41	L9522
Godwin, Clarence Arthur	RAF No. 745859	F/Sgt	24	RAF	24.07.41	L9527
Goodwin, Frederick Stanley	RAF No. 1499120	AC2	19	RAF	14.04.42	L9576
Gourley, William Henry James	Aus.402118	Sgt	23	RAAF	24.07.41	L9529
Grenyer, Alfred James	RAF No. 568042	Sgt	21	RAF	21.07.41	L9533
Grigg, Gerald Leonard	RAF No. 1165305	Sgt	21	RAF	11.12.41	L9600
Gurney, James Edward	RAF No. 527385	Sgt	26	RAF	14.04.42	L9576
Hall John Napier	RAF No. 743002	Sgt	n/k	RAF	13.01.41	L9487
Hammond, Albert Edward	RAF No. 535641	F/Sgt	n/k	RAF	09.07.41	L9521
Hancock, James Anthony	RAF No. 648598	Cpl	21	RAF	22.12.41	L9522
Hancock, Laurence	RAF No. 977649	Sgt	21	RAF	30.06.41	L9499
Hares, Richard Norman	RAF No. 1113461	Sgt	27	RAF	30.06.41	L9499
Heggie, Alistair Alexander Stobie	RAF No. 967663	Sgt	24	RAF	25.08.41	L9572
Heller, Albert James	RAF No. 552112	F/Sgt	20	RAF	26.07.41	L9507
Henry, Michael Thomas Gibson	RAF No. 39876	F/L	28	RAF	13.01.41	L9487
Hill, Frederick William	RAF No. 902598	Sgt	34	RAF	29.08.41	L9501
Hill, Roy William Joseph	RAF No. 551932	F/Sgt	20	RAF	24.07.41	L9517
Hogan, Edward Peter	RAF No. 940001	Sgt	n/k	RAF	13.08.41	L9562
Horner, Charles Henry	RAF No. 560615	F/Sgt	30	RAF	24.07.41	L9529
Howell, Alfred Thomas	RAF No. 1380271	Sgt	22	RAF	14.04.42	L9576
Howes, Albert John	RAF No. 920805	Sgt	n/k	RAF	21.07.41	L9533
Hudgell, Kenneth Napier	RAF No. 964546	Sgt	28	RAF	21.07.41	L9533
Hutchin, Ronald Edward	RAF No. 10449	P/O	23	RAF	14.09.41	L9567
Ingham, Percy	RAF No. 526092	Sgt	25	RAF	30.06.41	L9499
Isaac, Alexander Howard	RAF No. 1190773	Sgt	31	RAF	09.10.42	L9574
James, Ross	RAF No. 42062	F/O	28	RAF	03.09.41	L9508
Jesse, William Charles Browne	RAF No. 633777	Sgt	22	(IRE)/RAF	13.01.41	L9487
Johnson, John Rudolph	Can./ R.56089	Sgt	n/k	RCAF	31.10.41	L9602
Joshua, Frederick John	RAF No. 87041	F/O	29	RAF	14.04.42	L9576
Keighley, Colin George Coltham	RAF No. 1333962	AC1	20	RAF	14.04.42	L9576
Kent, Robert William George	RAF No. 559083	Sgt	41	RAF	11.12.41	L9600
Ketteringham, Laurence William	RAF No. 1153499	Sgt	21	RAF	11.12.41	L9600
Leach, Francis	RAF No. 113402	P/O	26	RAF	09.10.42	L9574
Lewin, Austin Ellerker	RAF No. 84304	F/L	n/k	RAF	24.07.41	L9529
Lisle, Ronald	RAF No.100618	P/O	n/k	RAF	15.08.41	L9500
Lucas, Reginald	RAF No. 741992	Sgt	29	RAF	10.03.41	L9487
Mahady, Thomas	RAF No. 1371443	AC1	n/k	RAF	14.04.42	L9576
Manley, Kenneth James Arthur	RAF No. 951350	Sgt	23	RAF	31.05.42	L9605
Manning, Alfred James	RAF No. 961238	Sgt	28	RAF	29.08.41	L9501
Markham, Vivian Maxwell	RAF No. 100032	P/O	n/k	RAF	25.08.41	L9572
Marks, Gilbert	RAF No. 1169564	Sgt	20	RAF	14.04.42	L9576
Mayes, Stanley Charles	RAF No. 755992	Sgt	21	RAF	13.08.41	L9562
Mayston, Stanley Robert	RAF No. 908800	Sgt	21	RAF	22.12.41	L9522
McDonald, Leslie Joseph	RAF No. 79513	P/O	23	(NZ)/RAF	13.01.41	L9487
McGregor-Cheers, Jack	RAF No. 64889	P/O	24	RAF	25.08.41	L9572
McHale, John	RAF No. 741064	F/Sgt	n/k	RAF	13.08.41	L9562
McHale, Thomas Percival	RAF No. 936804	Sgt	n/k	RAF	25.08.41	L9572
McInnes, Reginald James	Can./ R.60280	Sgt	21	RCAF	13.08.41	L9562
McKenna, Joseph Francis Patrick John	RAF No. 84395	P/O	24	RAF	24.07.41	L9517
McLean, Neil Frederick	NZ403876	P/O	26	RNZAF	31.10.41	L9602
McQuigg, Howard Torrens	RAF No. 575079	Sgt	19	RAF	15.08.41	L9500
Mennie, Douglas James	RAF No. 940550	Sgt	n/k	RAF	26.07.41	L9507
Merrifield, Leslie	RAF No. 702345	Sgt	23	RAF	22.12.41	L9522
Moir, Alastair Ian Taylor	RAF No. 137208	F/O	23	RAF	25.05.43	L9571

MUTTART, Elmer Bagnell	CAN./ R.64729	F/Sgt	n/k	RCAF	13.10.41	L9561
MYCOCK, James	RAF No. 1378898	Sgt	22	RAF	31.10.41	L9602
NEWSTEAD, Conrad Howard	RAF No. 567204	Sgt	24	RAF	24.07.41	L9527
NIVEN, Alexander Thompson	RAF No. 1325203	Sgt	n/k	RAF	13.08.41	L9530
O'BRIEN, Charles Stuart	CAN./ R.65254	F/Sgt	23	RCAF	31.10.41	L9602
OWEN, Robert Fenwick	RAF No. 84914	F/L	25	RAF	22.12.41	L9522
PARKES, Thomas Arthur	RAF No. 526677	Sgt	24	RAF	09.07.41	L9521
PEARSON, Charles James	RAF No. 64268	P/O	27	RAF	29.08.41	L9501
PILBEAM, John Mitchell	RAF No. 918421	Sgt	19	RAF	24.07.41	L9517
PLOWMAN, Francis Leslie	RAF No. 567918	Sgt	21	RAF	13.01.41	L9487
RICE, Leonard Thomas	RAF No. 518719	Sgt	25	RAF	24.07.41	L9517
ROBISON, Thomas Douglas Inglis	RAF No. 42768	F/L	23	(NZ)/RAF	30.06.41	L9499
ROGERS, John Johnston	RAF No. 966861	F/Sgt	n/k	RAF	15.08.41	L9500
ROSE, Alfred William	RAF No. 746835	Sgt	n/k	RAF	29.08.41	L9501
RUDLIN, Reginald Thomas	RAF No. 912084	Sgt	27	RAF	24.07.41	L9527
RUSSELL, Anthony Charles Henry Reid	RAF No. 904441	Sgt	22	RAF	13.01.41	L9487
SEWELL, Kenneth Randolph	RAF No.751350	Sgt	25	RAF	15.08.41	L9500
SHIRLEY, Sidney Harry James	RAF No. 804422	Sgt	32	RAF	24.07.41	L9527
SHORT, Ernest	RAF No. 567019	Sgt	23	RAF	26.07.41	L9507
SIMPSON, Alexander Urquart*	RAF No. 647593	Sgt	n/k	RAF	30.06.41	L9501
SLATER, Denis	RAF No. 755528	Sgt	20	RAF	03.09.41	L9560
SPENCER, Ernest James	RAF No. 903905	Sgt	36	RAF	14.04.42	L9576
STOBBS, Walter Kell	RAF No. 86396	P/O	22	RAF	24.06.41	L9492
STONE, Harold Walter*	RAF No. 45899	P/O	27	RAF	24.07.41	L9511
STROUD, Arthur Henry	RAF No. 909968	Sgt	n/k	RAF	03.09.41	L9560
SUMMERS, George	RAF No. 967240	Sgt	n/k	RAF	24.07.41	L9517
THOMAS, Eric Rees	RAF No. 618140	Sgt	20	RAF	08.11.41	L9603
THOMPSON, Herbert	RAF No. 1052413	Sgt	20	RAF	29.08.41	L9501
THOMPSON, Robert Ferguson	RAF No. 974372	Sgt	20	RAF	08.11.41	L9603
TURNER, Alan	RAF No. 570035	Sgt	n/k	RAF	24.06.41	L9492
VENESS, Daniel Edward	AUS.411620	F/Sgt	32	RAAF	25.05.43	L9571
VICKERY, Percy James	RAF No. 981272	Sgt	n/k	RAF	24.07.41	L9529
WAKELING, Maurice Victor	RAF No. 1152209	Sgt	26	RAF	11.12.41	L9600
WEST, James Gardner Simpson	RAF No. 517461	Sgt	26	RAF	13.08.41	L9562
WHITAKER, Gordon	RAF No. 45055	P/O	20	RAF	08.11.41	L9603
WHITFIELD, Clarence Emerson	RAF No. 923812	Sgt	21	RAF	13.08.41	L9531
WILLINGHAM, Norman	RAF No. 922470	Sgt	27	RAF	03.09.41	L9560
WOOD, Charles Edward	RAF No. 568343	Sgt	n/k	RAF	31.10.41	L9602
WOODS, William	RAF No. 531299	F/Sgt	26	(IRE)/RAF	13.08.41	L9530
YOUNG, John Kenneth	RAF No. 947403	Sgt	21	RAF	03.09.41	L9508

*Killed on board, but the aircraft made a safe return.

Total: 146

Australia: 2, Canada: 8, Ireland (Eire): 2, New Zealand: 2, United Kingdom: 132

n/k: not known

In Autumn 1941, 35 Sqn received a media visit. Here members were asked to pose for the photograph. On the right, standing, is David S. S. Wilkerson, later DSO, DFC, and who was killed in a flying accident as a Wing Commander in September 1944.

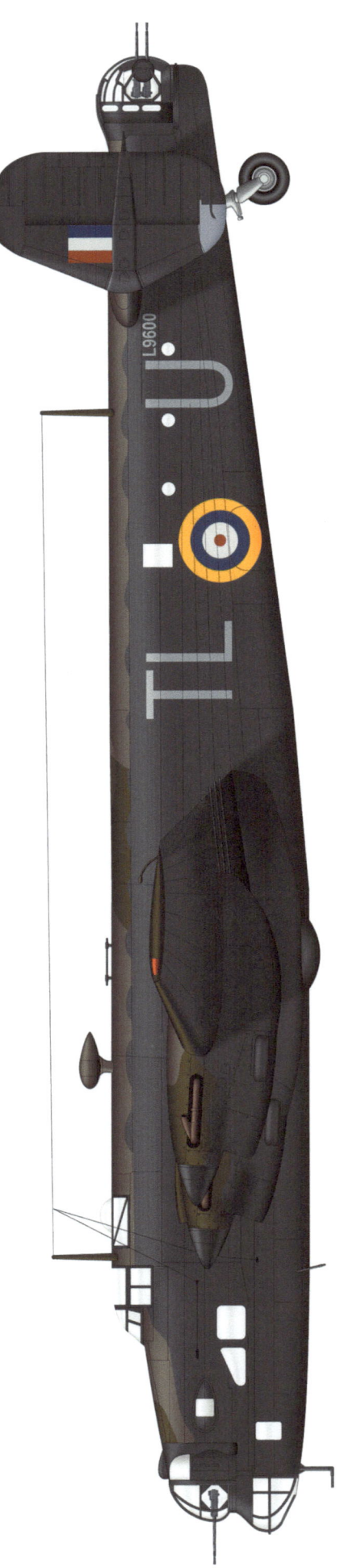

Handley Page Halifax Mk. I L9600
No. 35 Squadron
Linton-on-Ouse (UK), October 1941

Handley Page Halifax Mk. I L9530
No. 76 Squadron
Middleton St. George (UK), August 1941

SQUADRONS! - The series

1. The Supermarine Spitfire Mk VI
2. The Republic Thunderbolt Mk I
3. The Supermarine Spitfire Mk V in the Far East
4. The Boeing Fortress Mk I
5. The Supermarine Spitfire Mk XII
6. The Supermarine Spitfire Mk VII
7. The Supermarine Spitfire F. 21
8. The Handley Page Halifax Mk I
9. The Forgotten Fighters
10. The NA Mustang IV in Western Europe
11. The NA Mustang IV over the Balkans and Italy
12. The Supermarine Spitfire Mk XVI - *The British*
13. The Martin Marauder Mk I
14. The Supermarine Spitfire Mk VIII in the Southwest Pacific - *The British*
15. The Gloster Meteor F.I & F.III
16. The NA Mitchell - *The Dutch, Poles and French*
17. The Curtiss Mohawk
18. The Curtiss Kittyhawk Mk II
19. The Boulton Paul Defiant - *day and night fighter*
20. The Supermarine Spitfire Mk VIII in the Southwest Pacific - *The Australians*
21. The Boeing Fortress Mk II & Mk III
22. The Douglas Boston and Havoc - *The Australians*
23. The Republic Thunderbolt Mk II
24. The Douglas Boston and Havoc - *Night fighters*
25. The Supermarine Spitfire Mk V - *The Eagles*
26. The Hawker Hurricane - *The Canadians*
27. The Supermarine Spitfire Mk V - *The 'Bombay' squadrons*
28. The Consolidated Liberator - *The Australians*
29. The Supermarine Spitfire Mk XVI - *The Dominions*
30. The Supermarine Spitfire Mk V - *The Belgian and Dutch squadrons*
31. The Supermarine Spitfire Mk V - *The New-Zealanders*
32. The Supermarine Spitfire Mk V - *The Norwegians*
33. The Brewster Buffalo
34. The Supermarine Spitfire Mk II - *The Foreign squadrons*
35. The Martin Marauder Mk II
36. The Supermarine Spitfire Mk V - *The Special Reserve squadrons*
37. The Supermarine Spitfire Mk XIV - *The Belgian and Dutch squadrons*
38. The Supermarine Spitfire Mk II - *The Rhodesian, Dominion & Eagle squadrons*
39. The Douglas Boston and Havoc - *Intruders*
40. The North American Mustang Mk III over Italy and the Balkans (Pt-1)
41. The Bristol Brigand
42. The Supermarine Spitfire Mk V - *The Australians*
43. The Hawker Typhoon - *The Rhodesian squadrons*
44. The Supermarine Spitfire F.22 & F.24
45. The Supermarine Spitfire Mk IX - *The Belgian and Dutch squadrons*
46. The North American & CAC Mustang - *The RAAF*
47. The Westland Whirlwind
48. The Supermarine Spitfire Mk XIV - *The British squadrons*
49. The Supermarine Spitfire Mk I - *The beginning (the Auxiliary squadrons)*
50. The Hawker Tempest Mk V - *The New Zealanders*
51. The Last of the Long-Range Biplane Flying Boats
52. The Supermarine Spitfire Mk IX - *The Former Canadian Homefront squadrons*
53. The Hawker Hurricane Mk I & Mk II - *The Eagle squadrons*
54. The Hawker biplane fighters
55. The Supermarine Spitfire Mk IX - *The Auxiliary squadrons*
56. The Hawker Typhoon - *The Canadian squadrons*
57. The Douglas SBD - *New Zealand and France*
58. The Forgotten Patrol Seaplanes
59. The Dutch Fighter Squadrons - *Nos. 322 & 120 (NEI) Squadrons*
60. The Supermarine Spitfire - *The Australian Squadrons in Western Europe and the Med*
61. The Belgian Fighter Squadrons - *Nos. 349 & 350 Squadrons*
62. The Supermarine Spitfire Mk I - *The beginning (the Regular squadrons)*
63. The Hawker Typhoon - *The 'Fellowship of the Bellows' squadrons*
64. The North American Mustang Mk I & Mk II
65. The Eagle Squadrons *Nos. 71, 121 & 133 Squadrons*
66. The Handley Page Hampden *Torpedo-bomber*
67. The North American Mustang Mk III over Italy and the Balkans (Pt-2)
68. The Hawker Tempest Mk V - *The expansion*
69. The NA Mitchell - *The RAF in the Far East, the NEIAF and the RAAF*
70. The Supermarine Spitfire Mk XVI - *The definitive operational history 1944-1945*
71. The Curtiss Kittyhawk - *The Canadians*
72. The New Zealand day fighter squadrons in Europe - *Nos 485 & 486 Squadrons*
73. The Supermarine Spitfire Mk XIV - *The definitive operational history 1944-1945*

www.ingramcontent.com/pod-product-compliance
Lightning Source LLC
Chambersburg PA
CBHW060823090426
42738CB00002B/88